ADAPTING SOFTWARE DEVELOPMENT FOR
INNOVATION & EFFICIENCY

AYEBAKURO NGONAMONDI

Copyright © 2024 by **Ayebakuro Ngonamondi**

All rights reserved.

Adapting Software Development for Innovation and Efficiency

No part of this book may be reproduced or transmitted in any form or by any means, electronic or mechanical, including photocopying, recording, or by any information storage and retrieval system, without prior written permission from the copyright owner.

Any information in this book is for educational and informational purposes only. It should not be substituted for financial advice.

The author and publisher do not endorse any commercial products or services linked from other websites to this book.

Globally Available

ISBN: 978-4-3351-3954-3

A catalogue record of this book will be available from the National Library of Nigeria.

TABLE OF CONTENTS

FOREWORD iv

INTRODUCTION v

CHAPTER 1
INTRODUCTION TO SOFTWARE DEVELOPMENT IN A MODERN WORLD 1

CHAPTER 2
AGILE AND LEAN PRINCIPLES FOR SOFTWARE DEVELOPMENT 32

CHAPTER 3
INCORPORATING DEVOPS FOR CONTINOUS INNOVATION 47

CHAPTER4
SCALING SOFTWARE DEVELOPMENT THROUGH MICROSERVICES
ARCHITECTURE 56

CHAPTER 5
EMBRACING EMERGING TECHNOLOGIES FOR INNOVATION 70

CHAPTER.6
EFFECTIVE TEAM COLLABORATIONS AND COMMUNICATIONS 76

CHAPTER 7
USER-CENTRIC DESIGN AND INNOVATION 89

CHAPTER 8
SECURITY AS A FOUNDATION FOR INNOVATION 110

CHAPTER 9
SOFTWARE DEVELOPMENT METRICS AND PERFOMANCE OPTIMISATIONS 131

CHAPTER 10
FUTURE TRENDS IN SOFTWARE DEVELOPMENT 146

FOREWORD

Adapting Software Development for Innovation and Efficiency is a timely guide that explores the evolving landscape of modern software development. It emphasizes the importance of creativity, adaptability, and strategic thinking in addition to technical skills. The book covers traditional and modern development methodologies like Waterfall, Agile, and DevOps, while highlighting the role of technological advancements such as AI, cloud computing, and microservices in driving innovation.

Aimed at developers, project managers, and tech entrepreneurs, the book offers insights into how software can be developed efficiently while fostering innovation, positioning readers to lead in an ever-changing industry.

INTRODUCTION

In today's fast-paced, technology-driven world, software development plays an integral role in shaping the future of business, communication, and innovation. With the increasing demand for digital transformation across industries, the ability to adapt, innovate, and improve software development practices has become crucial. This book, Adapting Software Development for Innovation and Efficiency, explores how the field has evolved from traditional methodologies to modern, agile practices, while highlighting the essential skills, tools, and frameworks needed to stay ahead in this dynamic environment.

At its core, software development is not just about writing code or applying algorithms; it's about solving complex problems and delivering valuable solutions that drive business outcomes. This requires a deeper understanding of both the technical and strategic aspects of the development process. As the field evolves, developers and teams must adapt their approaches, upskill with new technologies, and foster a mindset of continuous learning and innovation.

Throughout this book, you'll explore a comprehensive view of software development, starting with its traditional roots and progressing to modern methodologies like Agile, DevOps, and continuous integration. We dive into key concepts such as product, process, and technological innovations that have reshaped the industry, as well as the role of business model innovation in revolutionizing how software is delivered and consumed. Furthermore, the book discusses future trends and the importance of adapting to new tools, frameworks, and approaches to remain relevant and competitive in the industry.

While technical expertise is undoubtedly vital, this book emphasizes the human elements—creativity, curiosity, and critical thinking—that allow developers to push boundaries, think strategically, and create software that not only functions but excels. You'll learn how to approach software development with a holistic mindset, seeing beyond the code to understand how each decision impacts the broader system, user experience, and business objectives.

Whether you're an experienced developer, a team leader, or someone just entering the software industry, this book provides practical insights and forward-looking perspectives on how to navigate the complexities of modern software development. The goal is to help you build more innovative, efficient, and scalable solutions that thrive in today's fast-moving digital landscape.

As we explore traditional methodologies, future trends, and the importance of continuous learning, you'll gain the tools and knowledge to adapt your software development practices, driving both innovation and efficiency. Let's embark on this journey to not only build better software but also to craft solutions that shape the future of technology and business.

CHAPTER 1

INTRODUCTION TO SOFTWARE DEVELOPMENT IN A MODERN WORLD

At first glance, software development might seem to be all about coding, frameworks, and algorithms. It's easy to think the most important skills a developer needs are purely technical—like proficiency in languages such as Python or Java, mastering version control, or understanding software architecture. These are, of course, essential parts of the job. Without technical know-how, it's hard to even start building software. However, focusing solely on these technical skills only tells part of the story. In reality, software development is much more than just writing code or applying best practices. The technical side is the foundation, but it's just the beginning. What truly sets successful developers apart is their mindset, their ability to think creatively, ask insightful questions, and approach problems with critical, strategic thinking.

In an ever-evolving field like software development, where technologies and methodologies are constantly shifting, a developer's mindset and adaptability become their greatest assets. Consider this scenario: two developers are given the same task of implementing a new feature. Both have access to the same tools and resources. One developer treats it as a straightforward technical task, writing code to meet the functional requirements. The other developer begins by questioning the requirements, exploring the feature's purpose, considering the user experience, and thinking about how it fits into the overall system. This second developer isn't just writing code, they are thinking strategically, curious about the broader picture, and analyzing potential challenges. This approach leads to more innovative, efficient, and scalable solutions.

Software development is often complex and uncertain. Developers frequently face challenges that don't have clear instructions or easy solutions. For example, projects may have conflicting requirements, tight deadlines, or incomplete documentation. Sometimes, the tools at hand may not be fully suitable for the task, forcing developers to look for alternatives or come up with new approaches. This is where creativity comes into play. A creative developer can navigate these constraints, finding innovative ways to solve problems and increase efficiency. They turn challenges into opportunities, using limitations as a springboard to craft unique, valuable solutions.

Curiosity is also an essential trait for developers. The best developers are those who constantly ask, "What if?" They don't settle for the first solution, they experiment, test, and explore different possibilities, driven by the desire to improve and innovate. Whether they're diving into the inner workings of a new technology or exploring ways to optimize a system, curious developers often find insights that others miss.

However, creativity and curiosity need to be paired with critical thinking. In a field where software impacts everything from business performance to public safety, developers must evaluate their decisions with careful, logical thinking. Whether assessing performance, ensuring security, or considering long-term maintenance, critical thinking ensures that solutions are robust, efficient, and aligned with project goals.

In the end, while technical expertise is vital in software development, true innovation and efficiency come from combining creativity, curiosity, and critical thinking. Developers who embrace these qualities push boundaries, solve complex problems, and create software that not only functions but excels in today's fast-moving world.

OVERVIEW OF TRADITIONAL SOFTWARE DEVELOPMENT METHODOLOGY

Traditional software development methodologies have been crucial in shaping how software systems are designed, built, and maintained. These methodologies have evolved over time, reflecting changes in technology, business needs, and team dynamics. Below is an extensive overview of the most widely adopted traditional methodologies in software development, which can broadly be categorized into linear, iterative, and incremental approaches.

A. WATERFALL METHODOLOGY

The Waterfall model is one of the earliest and most straightforward software development methodologies. It follows a linear and sequential approach where progress is seen as flowing steadily downwards (like a waterfall) through several phases. These phrases are:

Requirements gathering: All the system requirements are collected from the stakeholders and documented.

System design: The software architecture and system design are created based on the requirements.

Implementation: Developers write code to implement the design and translate it into working software.

Testing: The system is thoroughly tested to ensure it meets the required functionality and quality.

Deployment: The software is deployed in the production environment.

Maintenance: After deployment, any issues that arise are resolved, and updates or improvements are made.

ADVANTAGES

Simple and structured: Waterfall's well-defined stages and deliverables make it easy to understand and manage.

Clear milestones: Each phase must be completed before moving on to the next, ensuring that everything is in place before development proceeds.

Suitable for smaller projects: If the requirements are well-understood from the outset, this methodology works well, particularly for short-duration projects.

DISADVANTAGES:

Inflexibility: Once a phase is completed, it's challenging to make changes without starting over.

Delayed feedback: Testing occurs only after implementation, so problems can be discovered late in the process, making them costly to fix.

Not adaptive to change: If customer requirements evolve during development, the rigid structure of Waterfall makes it difficult to adapt without major rework.

B. V-MODEL (VERIFICATION AND VALIDATION MODEL)

The V-Model, or the Verification and Validation model, is an extension of the Waterfall model that emphasizes testing throughout the development lifecycle. Each development phase in the V-Model has a corresponding testing phase, forming a "V" shape in diagrams.

Each phase of development undergoes verification, and corresponding validation is conducted during testing. The idea is to detect issues as early as possible, reducing the cost and effort of fixing defects later in the development process.

ADVANTAGES

Early defect detection: By tying testing to each phase of development, defects are more likely to be caught early.

Well-structured: Like the Waterfall model, it provides a clear structure with defined deliverables at each stage.

Emphasis on testing: The focus on testing from the beginning of the project ensures a more robust final product.

DISADVANTAGES

Rigid structure: Similar to the Waterfall model, the V-Model is highly structured and not well-suited for projects where requirements may evolve over time.

Late working product: The final product only emerges after the entire development and testing cycle, leaving little room for iterative feedback.

C. INCREMENTAL MODEL

The Incremental model breaks down the software development process into smaller, more manageable parts called increments. Each increment builds upon the previous ones, gradually adding functionality to the system. At the end of each increment, a working version of the product is delivered. The project starts with the most critical requirements, with less important features developed in later increments.

Initial phase: Focuses on core functionality.

Subsequent increments: Gradually add more features and refine the system.

ADVANTAGES

Early delivery: Working software is delivered early in the process, allowing for feedback and adjustments.

Risk management: High-risk features are often addressed early, reducing the chance of failure.

Flexibility: Changes can be made in subsequent increments without affecting previous work.

DISADVANTAGES

Incomplete system: Each increment may only provide a partial solution until the final increment is completed, which could be challenging if the system needs to be fully operational early on.

Planning challenges: It can be challenging to plan the entire project upfront since each increment may reveal new challenges or requirements.

D. ITERATIVE DEVELOPMENT

Iterative development is a cyclical approach where the software is developed in iterations or versions. Each iteration involves planning, design, development, and testing phases, resulting in a working software version that is improved upon with each subsequent iteration.

Unlike the Incremental model, where new functionality is added in each iteration, the Iterative model focuses on improving and refining existing functionality. Feedback from users or testing results in adjustments being made in the next iteration.

ADVANTAGES

Continuous refinement: Software is continuously improved based on feedback and testing.

Early risk identification: Risks are identified early and can be addressed in future iterations.

Customer feedback: Frequent deliveries allow customers to see progress and provide input early and often.

DISADVANTAGES

Resource-intensive: Constant iterations can be resource-heavy, requiring significant time and effort from developers and testers.

Complexity management: Managing multiple iterations and changes can become complex, especially as the software grows in size and complexity.

E. SPIRAL MODEL

The Spiral model is a risk-driven approach that combines elements of both iterative and waterfall models. It breaks the project into several cycles or spirals, with each cycle involving planning, risk analysis, design, development, and testing. At the end of each cycle, stakeholders review the progress, and the decision is made on whether to proceed with the next phase or revisit a previous one.

The core idea of the Spiral model is risk management. Each cycle begins with identifying and resolving the most significant risks, making this approach suitable for large, complex, and high-risk projects.

ADVANTAGES

Risk management: The emphasis on early risk identification and mitigation reduces the chance of failure.

Flexibility: The project can be revisited and adjusted at any point, making it more adaptable to changing requirements.

Iterative improvements: The project evolves through iterations, allowing for continuous refinement and improvement.

DISADVANTAGES

High cost: The constant revisiting of phases can make this model more costly and time-consuming than others.

Complexity: The Spiral model can be difficult to manage, especially for smaller teams or less experienced project managers.

Requires strong management: Success with the Spiral model depends heavily on the ability of the project manager to manage risks and coordinate between cycles effectively.

F. RAD (RAPID APPLICATION DEVELOPMENT)

The Rapid Application Development (RAD) model focuses on quick development and iteration cycles, emphasizing user feedback and rapid prototyping. It involves the following stages:

Requirements planning: A quick gathering of the key requirements.

User design: Prototyping and user feedback are central during this stage.

Construction: Software is built quickly with user feedback incorporated continuously.

Cutover: The final product is tested, reviewed, and moved to production.

ADVANTAGES

Fast development: RAD's emphasis on quick iteration and prototyping speeds up the development process.

User involvement: Constant user feedback ensures the final product aligns closely with user needs and expectations.

Flexibility: Changes in requirements can be easily accommodated during the prototyping stages.

DISADVANTAGES

Not suitable for large projects: RAD is typically better suited for small to medium-sized projects due to its focus on speed and user feedback.

High user involvement needed: If users are not available or engaged, the process can stall.

Less emphasis on scalability: Speed is prioritized over long-term scalability or performance, which may result in technical debt in larger projects.

Traditional software development methodologies provide structured, well-established frameworks for building software systems. From the linear approach of Waterfall to the risk-driven Spiral model, each methodology offers distinct advantages and disadvantages. Choosing the right methodology depends on project size, complexity, requirements, and team dynamics. While these traditional methods have given way to more agile and adaptive approaches in modern software development, they still offer valuable insights and frameworks for specific types of projects, especially those with well-defined requirements and little need for frequent changes.

DEFINING INNOVATION IN THE CONTEXT OF SOFTWARE DEVELOPMENT

Innovation in software development is a multifaceted concept that transcends the mere creation of new applications or systems. It encompasses the process of introducing new ideas, methodologies, technologies, and solutions that enhance the way software is designed, developed, deployed, and maintained. Innovation in this context can take many forms, ranging from the adoption of cutting-edge tools and techniques to the reimagining of business processes or the development of novel software products that disrupt markets.

To fully understand innovation in software development, it's essential to explore its various dimensions, the drivers behind it, and the impact it has on the industry as a whole.

A. WHAT IS INNOVATION IN SOFTWARE DEVELOPMENT?

Innovation in software development refers to the introduction of new technologies, frameworks, architectures, processes, or methodologies that result in improved software quality, enhanced efficiency, and better alignment with user needs. It goes beyond simply making incremental improvements to existing solutions, it involves thinking creatively, breaking conventions, and delivering new or significantly improved capabilities.

Innovation in software development refers to the introduction of new technologies, frameworks, architectures, processes, or methodologies that result in improved software quality, enhanced efficiency, and better alignment with user needs. It goes beyond simply making incremental improvements to existing solutions, it involves thinking creatively, breaking conventions, and delivering new or significantly improved capabilities.

In software development, innovation isn't limited to grand breaking throughs, it can also involve more incremental but meaningful improvements that collectively enhance productivity, performance, and quality.

B. DIMENSIONS OF INNOVATION IN SOFTWARE DEVELOPMENT

i. Product Innovation

Product innovation in software development involves the creation of entirely new software solutions or significant upgrades to existing ones. These innovations are often driven by changing user demands, market opportunities, or advances in technology. Product innovation can take several forms:

Disruptive products: These are breakthrough software applications that change the landscape of an industry or solve problems in completely new ways. Examples include the rise of mobile apps, cloud-based software services, and AI-driven platforms.

Feature enhancements: Existing software products may be enhanced with new functionalities or features that differentiate them from competitors and meet evolving customer needs.

Software as a Service (SaaS): The transition from traditional software products to cloud-based SaaS solutions is a form of product innovation that has fundamentally changed how users' access and interact with software.

Examples of product innovation

The introduction of Salesforce, which revolutionized customer relationship management (CRM) by offering a cloud-based SaaS platform.

Slack, which transformed workplace communication by creating a unified, searchable communication platform that replaced inefficient email threads.

ii. Process Innovation

Process innovation refers to the implementation of new methods for developing, testing, or delivering software. These innovations often focus on improving efficiency, reducing costs, or increasing the speed of development without compromising quality.

Process Innovation Can Be Seen In:

Agile and DevOps methodologies: These approaches transformed the way software is developed and delivered, emphasizing collaboration, iterative development, continuous integration, and faster deployment cycles.

Continuous integration and continuous deployment (CI/CD): Automation of software testing and deployment allows for more frequent updates and faster time to market.

Test automation: Automating the testing process, particularly regression testing, ensures higher quality software by identifying defects earlier in the development lifecycle.

Examples of Process Innovation:

DevOps, which integrates software development and IT operations to shorten the development lifecycle, improve collaboration, and deliver software more frequently.

The introduction of Agile methodologies, which replaced the traditional, rigid Waterfall model with iterative, flexible development cycles, enabling faster response to changing requirements and customer feedback.

iii. Technological Innovation

Technological innovation involves adopting or creating new technologies that enable the development of more advanced, efficient, or scalable software. These innovations often emerge as new programming languages, frameworks, or tools that allow developers to solve problems in novel ways.

KEY AREAS OF TECHNOLOGICAL INNOVATION INCLUDE

Artificial intelligence (AI) and machine learning (ML): Integrating AI/ML into software systems has led to smarter applications that can adapt to user behavior, automate decision-making, and offer predictive analytics.

Cloud computing: Cloud platforms, like AWS, Azure, and Google Cloud, have enabled developers to build and scale applications more efficiently, without the need for extensive on-premise infrastructure.

Microservices architecture: This approach to software development allows complex applications to be broken down into smaller, loosely coupled services that can be developed, deployed, and scaled independently.

Examples of technological innovation:

Serverless computing: Platforms like AWS Lambda allow developers to run code without managing server infrastructure, enabling faster development and reducing costs.

AI-driven chatbots: Innovations in natural language processing (NLP) have enabled the development of sophisticated chatbots that can interact with users in a more human-like manner, offering support, advice, or assistance in real time.

C. Business Model Innovation

Business model innovation in software development involves creating new ways of delivering, selling, or monetizing software solutions. This type of innovation often reflects changes in customer expectations, technological advances, or market dynamics.

Examples include:

Subscription-based models: The shift from one-time software purchases to subscription-based models (SaaS) has allowed companies to offer continuous value to customers through regular updates and support.

Freemium models: Offering basic software features for free, while charging for premium features or advanced functionality, has become a popular way to attract a broad user base and convert a percentage of them into paying customers.

Open-source software: Open-source business models, where software is freely available for anyone to use, contribute to, or modify, have fostered communities of developers and encouraged widespread adoption and collaboration.

Examples of Business Model Innovation:

GitHub, which initially allowed developers to host code repositories for free and later introduced premium subscription plans for private repositories and additional features.

Red Hat and its success with open-source software, offering enterprise-level support and services around its Linux distribution while keeping the core product open-source.

D. Drivers of Innovation in Software Development

Several factors drive innovation in software development:

i. Technological Advancements

New technologies often serve as the catalyst for innovation. Advances in areas like AI, cloud computing, block chain, and mobile development provide new tools and frameworks that developers can use to create more powerful and flexible software.

ii. Market Demand

As customer needs and expectations evolve, software developers must innovate to remain competitive. Companies need to anticipate market trends, such as the shift to mobile-first solutions or the growing demand for personalized user experiences and develop innovative software to meet those demands.

iii. Competition

The competitive nature of the software industry often forces companies to innovate rapidly. Companies that fail to innovate risk being overtaken by competitors that offer superior products or more efficient processes.

iv. Regulatory Changes

Legal and regulatory changes can prompt innovation, especially in areas like security, data privacy (e.g., GDPR), and accessibility. Developers are often required to create new solutions or modify existing systems to comply with these regulations.

v. Globalization and Remote Work

The rise of remote work, accelerated by the COVID-19 pandemic, has driven innovation in collaboration tools and platforms. Software that enables real-time collaboration, secure data sharing, and virtual team management has become essential for businesses operating across different geographies.

E. Impact of Innovation on Software Development

Innovation in software development has far-reaching impacts, including:

Increased Productivity: Innovations such as automation, DevOps, and CI/CD pipelines streamline workflows, allowing teams to deliver higher-quality software more efficiently.

Faster Time-to-Market: By adopting agile methodologies, continuous deployment, and other innovations, software companies can respond quickly to changing market conditions and customer needs.

Improved Software Quality: Innovations in testing automation, AI-driven error detection, and other tools help developers identify and fix issues early in the development process, leading to more reliable and robust software.

Enhanced User Experience: Innovations in UX design, AI-driven personalization, and mobile-first development result in software that is more intuitive, accessible, and tailored to individual users.

Innovation in software development is the driving force behind the rapid evolution of the industry. Whether through the creation of groundbreaking products, the adoption of more efficient processes, the leveraging of new technologies, or the reinvention of business models, innovation plays a critical role in shaping the future of software. Developers and organizations that embrace innovation not only stay competitive but also push the boundaries of what's possible, creating software that better serves the needs of users, businesses, and society as a whole.

THE GROWING NEED FOR EFFICIENCY IN SOFTWARE PROJECTS

The growing need for efficiency in software projects has become a crucial factor in today's fast-paced, technology-driven world. Software development is an integral part of business operations, product innovations, and digital transformations across industries. With companies depending heavily on software to manage critical functions and delivering solutions to their customers, ensuring efficient project execution is no longer a luxury, it is a necessity.

THE IMPORTANCE OF EFFICIENCY IN SOFTWARE PROJECTS

Efficiency in software projects refers to the ability to maximize output (quality software) with minimum wasted effort or expense (time, resources, and costs). In the highly competitive environment of software development, teams are often pressured to deliver functional, scalable, and secure products under tight deadlines while ensuring quality and minimizing costs. Inefficient processes or mismanagement of resources can lead to delays, budget overruns, and subpar products, which in turn affect a company's competitiveness and reputation.

Software projects are also becoming more complex, involving diverse teams spread across geographies, multiple stakeholders, and a variety of tools and methodologies. In such an environment, efficiency means not only delivering projects on time but also ensuring smooth communication, collaboration, and agile decision-making to adapt to changing project requirements.

FACTORS DRIVING THE NEED FOR GREATER EFFICIENCY

i. Market Demands: Customers today demand faster updates, enhanced functionalities, and seamless experiences. To stay relevant, companies must constantly innovate, releasing new software versions or updates with minimal delays. Efficiency in managing code, testing, and deployment cycles becomes critical to meet these expectations without compromising on quality.

ii. Rapid Technological Advancements: The rise of new technologies like artificial intelligence, machine learning, and blockchain has led to a surge in demand for new software capabilities. Integrating these technologies into existing systems or creating entirely new platforms from scratch requires efficient workflows to avoid long development cycles and ensure timely implementation.

iii. Remote Work and Global Teams: With remote work becoming more common, many software teams now operate across multiple time zones and cultural contexts. Efficient collaboration tools, project management practices, and communication channels are necessary to ensure that the dispersed teams work harmoniously and productively toward common project goals.

iv. Agile and DevOps Methodologies: The adoption of agile methodologies and DevOps practices has revolutionized software development, shifting the focus toward continuous integration and delivery. These approaches require a high level of coordination between development and operations teams, as well as efficient feedback loops and automated testing environments to maintain fast release cycles without introducing bugs or security risks.

v. Cost Efficiency and Budget Constraints: As businesses grow, they often face increased pressure to control costs while maintaining high-quality software solutions. Efficient management of development resources, such as personnel and tools, can lead to substantial cost savings. This has led to the proliferation of tools that aid in optimizing resource allocation, automating mundane tasks, and tracking progress in real time to prevent budget overruns.

CHALLENGES HINDERING EFFICIENCY

i. Despite the growing need for efficiency, several challenges can hinder progress in software projects:

ii. Poor Requirement Gathering: Inefficient requirement gathering can result in misunderstandings between stakeholders and developers, leading to wasted development time and resources on features that do not align with business needs.

iii. Inadequate Testing: Insufficient or inefficient testing practices can lead to bugs and security vulnerabilities that require costly post-release fixes. An efficient software development process integrates continuous testing to catch issues early in the development cycle.

iv. Misaligned Team Dynamics: In any collaborative project, team dynamics play a significant role in efficiency. Miscommunication, unclear roles, or a lack of collaboration can lead to bottlenecks, duplicated efforts, or errors that slow down progress.

STRATEGIES FOR IMPROVING EFFICIENCY

i. Automation: One of the most powerful tools to boost efficiency is the automation of repetitive tasks. This includes automated testing, continuous integration/continuous deployment (CI/CD) pipelines, and even using AI-driven tools for code generation and debugging. Automation allows developers to focus on more strategic tasks and reduces the margin for human error.

ii. Agile and Scrum Methodologies: Implementing agile methodologies like Scrum helps improve efficiency by breaking down projects into manageable sprints, allowing teams to continuously assess progress and make necessary adjustments. Agile fosters collaboration, flexibility, and faster delivery of incremental updates, which can reduce the risk of project delays.

iii. Clear Communication and Documentation: Establishing clear communication channels and thorough documentation practices ensure that everyone is involved in the project—whether developers, managers, or stakeholders—is aligned. This reduces the chances of miscommunication, scope creep, and mismanagement, which often lead to inefficiencies.

iv. Continuous Integration and Delivery (CI/CD): By adopting CI/CD practices, teams can streamline the process of code integration, testing, and deployment, enabling them to detect and address issues early. This leads to a smoother development cycle and significantly cuts down the time required for manual testing and deployment.

v. Resource Management: Efficient resource allocation can have a dramatic impact on project outcomes. By using project management tools that track time, progress, and resource utilization, project managers can ensure that each team member is utilized optimally. Additionally, balancing workloads and preventing burnout can lead to more sustainable productivity.

vi. Cross-functional Teams: Building cross-functional teams that include developers, designers, testers, and operations specialists can enhance efficiency by reducing handoffs between teams. This integrated approach ensures that all aspects of the project are considered and addressed early in the process, preventing issues from being overlooked.

THE ROLE OF TECHNOLOGY IN DRIVING EFFICIENCY

Technological advancements continue to play a key role in enhancing efficiency in software projects. Tools like version control systems (Git), project management platforms (Jira, Trello), and collaboration tools (Slack, Microsoft Teams) provide a centralized platform for managing workflows, tracking progress, and ensuring accountability. Cloud-based development environments, such as AWS, Microsoft Azure, or Google Cloud, further contribute to efficiency by allowing teams to collaborate in real time, access scalable resources, and automate infrastructure management.

Additionally, the use of artificial intelligence (AI) and machine learning (ML) in software development is growing. AI can assist with automated code reviews, testing, and even predicting project outcomes based on past data. ML models can be trained to optimize resource allocation, improve bug detection, and suggest refactorings, all of which contribute to more efficient project management.

HOW INNOVATION AND EFFICIENCY DRIVE SUCCESS IN TODAY'S COMPETITIVE BUSINESS LANDSCAPE

In today's highly competitive business landscape, innovation and efficiency are the twin engines that propel companies to success. Businesses, large and small, operate in an environment where change is constant, technology is rapidly advancing, and customer expectations continue to evolve. To stay relevant and outperform competitors, organizations must not only innovate but also achieve high levels of efficiency. These two elements are deeply intertwined; one cannot sustain innovation without efficiency, and efficient processes often lead to new avenues for innovation. Let's explore how these factors drive success in modern business.

THE ROLE OF INNOVATION

A. Staying Relevant

Innovation is the foundation of longevity in business. Companies that fail to innovate become stagnant and are quickly outpaced by more agile competitors. In industries ranging from technology to retail, the market leaders are often those who embrace change and continually develop new products, services, and methods of operation. Innovation helps businesses adapt to market shifts, meet new customer demands, and respond to the challenges posed by new competitors or disruptive technologies.

A striking example is the technology sector, where giants like Apple, Google, and Tesla have consistently innovated, not only maintaining their relevance but setting new industry standards. Apple's introduction of the iPhone revolutionized the smartphone industry, while Tesla has redefined the automotive market through electric vehicles and autonomous driving technologies. These companies thrive because they prioritize forward-thinking innovation, staying one step ahead of customer needs.

B. Creating New Markets

Innovation is not just about improving existing processes or products. It is also about creating entirely new markets and revenue streams. Think about companies like Uber or Airbnb. These businesses didn't merely improve upon traditional industries (taxis or hotels); they disrupted them by creating entirely new platforms and business models that connect consumers and service providers in ways never seen before. By doing so, they opened up new market opportunities that did not exist before.

C. Attracting and Retaining Talent

In today's knowledge-driven economy, businesses depend heavily on their human capital to drive innovation. The most talented employees seek out companies that are known for their innovative culture. Talented workers want to be part of organizations that invest in the future, develop new ideas, and allow them the space to be creative. By fostering a culture of innovation, businesses can attract the best talent, leading to a virtuous cycle of further innovation.

D. Fostering Customer Loyalty

Innovation can also enhance customer loyalty by delivering unique experiences or solving problems in new and better ways. Consumers today are more informed and have higher expectations than ever before. They demand more personalized, efficient, and innovative products and services. Companies that meet these demands through cutting-edge solutions stand a better chance of retaining their customer base and creating long-term loyalty.

THE ROLE OF EFFICIENCY

A. Cost Reduction

Efficiency in business refers to the optimal use of resources to achieve the best possible outcomes. One of the most significant benefits of efficiency is cost reduction. Streamlined processes, automation, and efficient resource allocation help businesses reduce overhead and production costs. This reduction in costs translates into higher profit margins or lower prices for consumers, which enhances competitiveness.

In manufacturing, for example, lean methodologies and automation have dramatically improved efficiency. Companies such as Toyota have implemented Just-In-Time (JIT) production to reduce waste and increase operational efficiency, which has helped the company remain profitable and competitive globally.

B. Increased Productivity

Efficiency is closely linked with productivity. The more efficient a business is, the more output it can generate from the same input. Increased productivity allows businesses to meet growing demand without having to proportionally increase costs. For instance, by leveraging technology such as artificial intelligence (AI), machine learning, and automation, businesses can streamline operations, improve decision-making, and enhance customer service, all of which lead to higher productivity.

E-commerce giants like Amazon are prime examples of this. Through highly efficient supply chains, robotics in warehouses, and data-driven logistics management, Amazon can deliver millions of products worldwide quickly and at low cost, all while maintaining strong profit margins.

C. Agility and Speed

Efficiency also allows businesses to be more agile. In a fast-paced, competitive environment, the ability to quickly adapt to changes or launch new products can be a significant competitive advantage. Efficient processes and well-organized teams make businesses more flexible, enabling rapid responses to market changes or customer feedback. This agility can be crucial in industries where trends and consumer preferences change rapidly, such as fashion, tech, or entertainment.

D. Customer Satisfaction

Efficiency can significantly impact customer satisfaction. In the age of instant gratification, consumers expect businesses to deliver products or services quickly and with minimal hassle. An efficient customer service system, for example, can resolve issues quickly, leading to higher levels of customer satisfaction and loyalty. Similarly, efficient logistics and supply chain management ensure timely delivery of goods, which is a key driver of customer retention in sectors like e-commerce or food delivery.

THE SYNERGY BETWEEN INNOVATION AND EFFICIENCY

While both innovation and efficiency are important in their own right, their true power lies in how they complement each other. Efficiency creates the foundation for sustained innovation by freeing up resources, time, money, and human capital that can be reinvested into research, development, and creative pursuits. Without efficient processes, businesses would struggle to scale innovative ideas, leading to wasted resources and reduced profitability.

At the same time, innovation can drive new efficiencies. Emerging technologies like AI, blockchain, and cloud computing are helping businesses not only innovate in terms of products and services but also reimagine their operations. AI, for example, is being used to analyze large datasets, automate routine tasks, and optimize supply chains, all of which contribute to more efficient and effective operations.

CASE STUDIES OF SUCCESS DRIVEN BY INNOVATION AND EFFICIENCY

i. Apple

Apple is often cited as a prime example of a company that excels in both innovation and efficiency. The company is known for its groundbreaking products such as the iPhone, iPad, and MacBook, all of which revolutionized their respective markets. However, Apple's success is also due to its efficient supply chain and production processes, which allow the company to deliver high-quality products on a scale.

ii. Tesla

Tesla's success is driven by its ability to innovate in the electric vehicle market while maintaining operational efficiency. Tesla's battery technology, autonomous driving features, and over-the-air software updates have set it apart as an innovator. However, its focus on vertical integration and efficient manufacturing processes has allowed it to lower costs and increase profitability, positioning Tesla as the market leader in electric vehicles.

iii. Amazon

Amazon has built its empire on the pillars of innovation and efficiency. From its innovative Prime membership model to its groundbreaking work in cloud computing with Amazon Web Services (AWS), the company has consistently pushed the boundaries of what's possible. On the efficient side, Amazon has pioneered new logistics and supply chain processes that allow for rapid delivery, giving it a competitive edge in the e-commerce market.

In the dynamic and competitive business landscape of today, innovation and efficiency are not just complementary; they are essential. Innovation keeps a business relevant and allows it to capture new markets, while efficiency ensures that resources are optimized, costs are controlled, and the business can scale profitably. Together, they form a potent combination that drives success, helping businesses not just survive but thrive in an ever-changing marketplace. Companies that master the balance between these two forces will continue to lead in their industries and shape the future of business.

CHAPTER 2

AGILE AND LEAN PRINCIPLES FOR SOFTWARE DEVELOPMENT

In the fast-paced world of software development, the demand for high-quality products delivered rapidly has led to the widespread adoption of methodologies that emphasize flexibility, efficiency, and collaboration. Among these methodologies, Agile and Lean principles have gained significant traction, reshaping how development teams work and responding to the ever-changing landscape of customer needs, market demands, and technological advancements. This chapter delves into the core principles of Agile and Lean, their evolution, and how they have transformed the software development process.

WHAT IS AGILE SOFTWARE DEVELOPMENT?

Agile software development is an approach to building software that emphasizes flexibility, collaboration, and customer-focused iteration. It involves breaking the development process into small, manageable cycles known as "sprints," which typically last 1-4 weeks. Each sprint delivers a working piece of the software that can be tested and improved based on user feedback.

Agile values individuals and interactions over processes and tools, working software over comprehensive documentation, customer collaboration over contract negotiation, and responding to change over following a plan. Agile methodologies include frameworks like Scrum, Kanban, and XP (Extreme Programming). This approach allows teams to adapt quickly to changes and deliver high-quality products in less time.

OVERVIEW OF AGILE PRINCIPLES

Agile is a mindset and set of practices designed to promote flexibility and continuous delivery in software development. It originated with the publication of the Agile Manifesto in 2001, which outlines four core values and twelve guiding principles that shape how teams should work to create high-quality software efficiently. The key values of Agile are:

Individuals and interactions over processes and tools

Agile places a strong emphasis on communication and collaboration between team members and stakeholders. While processes and tools are important, they should not overshadow the human element in software development.

Working software over comprehensive documentation

Agile promotes the delivery of functional software at regular intervals. Documentation is important, but it should not be so detailed or burdensome that it impedes the actual progress of building software.

Customer collaboration over contract negotiation

Instead of rigidly adhering to contractual terms, Agile teams work closely with customers and stakeholders throughout the development process, ensuring that the final product aligns with their evolving needs.

Responding to change over following a plan

Agile embraces change, whether it's in response to new customer feedback, technological advancements, or other external factors. The ability to pivot and adapt is a fundamental strength of the Agile methodology.

These values are supported by twelve principles that guide Agile teams in their day-to-day work. Some of the most notable principles include:

i. Deliver working software frequently, with a preference for shorter timescales (often in increments of 1 to 4 weeks).

ii. Welcome changing requirements, even late in development. Agile processes harness change for the customer's competitive advantage.

iii. Build projects around motivated individuals, giving them the environment and support they need and trusting them to get the job done.

iv. The most efficient and effective method of conveying information is face-to-face conversation.

v. Simplicity, the art of maximizing the amount of work not done—is essential.

KEY AGILE METHODOLOGIES

Agile is not a single methodology but a collection of frameworks that embody its principles. Among the most popular Agile methodologies are:

A. SCRUM

Scrum is one of the most widely used Agile frameworks. It is built around short, iterative cycles called "sprints," typically lasting 2 to 4 weeks. During each sprint, the team works to deliver a potentially shippable product increment. Scrum emphasizes transparency, inspection, and adaptation through a set of well-defined roles, events, and artifacts.

Roles: The key roles in Scrum are the Product Owner, Scrum Master, and the Development Team. The Product Owner is responsible for defining the product backlog (a prioritized list of features and requirements). The Scrum Master ensures the team adheres to Scrum practices and removes any impediments. The Development Team is responsible for delivering the work during each sprint.

Events: Scrum's core events include the Sprint Planning meeting (where the team decides what to work on during the sprint), Daily Scrum (a short daily meeting to review progress), Sprint Review (where the team demonstrates the completed work), and Sprint Retrospective (where the team reflects on what went well and what could be improved).

Artifacts: Scrum teams use key artifacts such as the Product Backlog, Sprint Backlog, and Increment. These help to ensure transparency and provide a clear picture of progress and work to be done.

B. KANBAN

Kanban is another popular Agile framework, originating from Lean manufacturing practices. It is designed to optimize workflow by visualizing tasks on a Kanban board. Each task moves through stages, from "to do" to "in progress" to "done," ensuring transparency and accountability within the team. Kanban emphasizes continuous delivery and focuses on limiting the amount of work in progress (WIP) at any given time.

Kanban is particularly well-suited for teams that need flexibility and have projects with unpredictable workloads. It doesn't rely on fixed-length sprints like Scrum, but instead, tasks are continuously worked on as capacity allows, making it ideal for maintenance or support teams.

OVERVIEW OF LEAN PRINCIPLES

Lean principles, originally derived from Toyota's manufacturing processes, have been adapted to software development under the concept of Lean Software Development. The Lean approach emphasizes the elimination of waste (anything that does not add value to the customer), continuous learning, and delivering value to the customer as quickly as possible.

The seven core principles of Lean Software Development are:

i. Eliminate Waste

Waste refers to any activity that doesn't add value to the end customer. In software development, this could include redundant code, unnecessary documentation, excessive meetings, or delays in the development pipeline. Lean teams strive to identify and eliminate waste at every stage of the process.

ii. Amplify Learning

Learn encourages continuous learning through experimentation, fast feedback, and iteration. Rather than waiting until the end of a long development cycle, Lean teams seek to learn from small increments of work and adjust based on the feedback they receive.

iii. Decide as Late as Possible

In rapidly changing environments, making decisions too early can lead to incorrect assumptions and wasted effort. Lean suggests delaying decisions until the last responsible moment, allowing teams to gather as much relevant information as possible before committing.

iv. Deliver as Fast as Possible

Lean teams aim to deliver software quickly and in small increments. Fast delivery ensures that customers receive value early and can provide feedback that informs future iterations.

v. Empower the Team

Lean emphasizes the importance of empowering development teams to make decisions and take ownership of the product. This approach fosters innovation, accountability, and faster problem-solving.

vi. Build Integrity In

Software integrity means that the product performs as expected and is maintainable over time. Lean promotes practices such as automated testing, continuous integration, and refactoring to ensure that quality is built into the product from the start, rather than bolted on at the end.

vii. Optimize the Whole

Lean focuses on optimizing the entire system, rather than just individual components. This principle encourages collaboration across different departments and teams, ensuring that everyone is aligned toward the same goal: delivering value to the customer.

The Synergy Between Agile and Lean

While Agile and Lean originated in different contexts, Agile in software development and lean in manufacturing their principles complement each other in many ways. Both emphasize delivering value to the customer, reducing waste, and being responsive to change. The main distinction lies in their focus: Agile is more concerned with adaptability and collaboration, while Lean is primarily focused on efficiency and the elimination of waste.

Together, they provide a powerful framework for modern software development teams.

For example, Lean's principle of delivering fast aligns perfectly with Agile's emphasis on short, iterative cycles of work. Meanwhile, Agile's focus on continuous feedback complements Lean's goal of amplifying learning. By combining Agile's adaptability with Lean's efficiency, development teams can create a sustainable and productive environment that encourages both innovation and consistent delivery.

CASE STUDIES: AGILE AND LEAN IN ACTION

a. Spotify: Scaling Agile for Innovation

Spotify has become a model for scaling Agile practices across large organizations. The company uses a framework called Spotify Model, which divides its development teams into small, cross-functional units known as squads. Each squad operates independently, following Agile principles like self-organization and iterative delivery. Additionally, Spotify uses Lean concepts to reduce waste and ensure smooth communication across teams, particularly when multiple squads collaborate on larger projects.

b Toyota: Lean in Software Development

Toyota, the originator of Lean manufacturing, has applied Lean principles to its software development processes. Toyota's IT departments use Kanban boards to manage workflows, reduce bottlenecks, and ensure continuous delivery of software updates. The company's emphasis on building quality is aligned with Lean principles, ensuring that software products are reliable, efficient, and meet customer expectations.

Agile and Lean principles have fundamentally changed how software is developed, focusing on flexibility, efficiency, and delivering value to the customer as quickly as possible. While Agile emphasizes collaboration, adaptability, and rapid feedback, Lean focuses on eliminating waste, continuous improvement, and optimizing the entire development process. Together, they create a powerful framework that drives productivity, innovation, and customer satisfaction in today's fast-paced software development landscape. By understanding and applying these principles, development teams can not only meet the demands of today's competitive market but also build the foundation for long-term success.

INCREASING EFFICIENCY THROUGH ITIRATIVE DEVELOPMENT AND CONTINUOUS IMPROVEMENTS!

Increasing efficiency through iterative development and continuous improvement is one of the core principles of Agile software development. This approach transforms traditional software development, which often followed rigid, long-term planning and extensive documentation before delivering a final product. In contrast, iterative development focuses on delivering smaller, functional increments of a product in short cycles or sprints. Each cycle is followed by a period of review, reflection, and adaptation. This process, combined with a mindset of continuous improvement, enables teams to enhance efficiency, respond rapidly to changes, and deliver higher-quality software faster.

KEY ASPECTS OF ITERATIVE DEVELOPMENT

i. Small, Incremental Releases: Iterative development breaks down the overall project into smaller pieces that can be completed in a short time frame (usually 1 to 4 weeks). These are known as increments, and each iteration results in a working product, even if it's just a subset of the final feature set. By developing in smaller increments, the team can focus on delivering real value early in the process, allowing users to begin interacting with and testing the software before it's fully finished. This "early delivery" prevents many of the pitfalls of waiting months or even years to discover issues.

ii. Frequent Feedback: After each sprint, the development team reviews the increment with stakeholders or customers, gathering valuable feedback. This enables early detection of flaws or unmet needs. With frequent input, teams can immediately adjust priorities, change requirements, or fix issues, minimizing wasted effort and maximizing efficiency. As the project evolves, the software closely aligns with user needs, and the team can continuously refine both the product and its development processes.

iii. Reduced Risk: By delivering software iteratively, the development team significantly reduces risk. Large, monolithic projects often encounter delays or failures because they attempt to deliver an entire product all at once. In contrast, iterative development ensures that if challenges arise, they are detected and addressed early, without risking the entire project. This early detection allows teams to pivot if necessary, adapting the software to changing needs, market demands, or technical constraints.

iv. Tightened Focus and Prioritization: Iterative development helps teams focus on what's most important, often utilizing a prioritized backlog of tasks. With a limited scope per sprint, developers can concentrate on delivering the most critical features first. This focus ensures that the development effort directly ties to business value and user requirements, eliminating unnecessary work on lower-priority features that may never be used.

CONTINUOUS IMPROVEMENT: THE KEY TO LONG-TERM EFFICIENCY

a. Regular Reflection: Continuous improvement is a practice in which teams regularly reflect on their work and processes to identify areas for improvement. Agile teams hold retrospectives at the end of each sprint to discuss what went well, what didn't, and what could be improved. This feedback loop fosters a culture of learning and adaptation, driving the team toward greater efficiency over time. By making small, incremental improvements in how they work, teams enhance productivity, reduce errors, and streamline communication.

b. Data-Driven Adjustments: Many Agile teams use metrics to measure performance during each iteration, such as velocity (how much work was completed), defect rates, or cycle times. These metrics provide actionable insights into how efficiently the team is working. For instance, if a team consistently misses sprint goals, this data can trigger a deeper investigation into the causes—whether it's over-committing, technical debt, or communication gaps. Based on these findings, the team can adjust their approach in future sprints, ensuring they are continuously fine-tuning their processes.

c. Collaboration and Communication: Efficiency in Agile isn't just about writing code faster, it's also about improving the way teams collaborate and communicate. Agile fosters a collaborative environment where developers, testers, designers, and product owners work closely together. By improving communication, Agile teams reduce misunderstandings, bottlenecks, and delays. Regular meetings like daily stand-ups ensure that everyone is on the same page and issues are addressed promptly. This ongoing collaboration is essential for achieving continuous improvement in both the software and the development process.

d. Embracing Change: One of Agile' s most important principles is welcoming changing requirements, even late in development. This might sound counterintuitive to efficiency, but by embracing change, Agile teams can avoid spending time on features or requirements that may no longer be relevant. Continuous improvement means being flexible enough to change course when better ideas emerge, market demands shift, or user feedback suggests a different direction. This adaptability prevents the wasted effort of building features that are no longer valuable, ensuring that development efforts stay focused on what matters most.

TOOLS AND TECHNIQUES FOR ITERATIVE DEVELOPMENT AND CONTINUOUS IMPROVEMENT

i. Scrum and Sprint Planning: Scrum is one of the most popular frameworks for applying Agile principles. It involves organizing work into time-boxed sprints, with each sprint focusing on a specific set of deliverables. Scrum teams hold regular ceremonies like sprint planning, daily stand-ups, sprint reviews, and retrospectives to ensure continuous improvement. In sprint planning, the team selects items from the backlog based on priority and team capacity, ensuring they only commit to what can be delivered within the sprint.

ii. Kanban for Flow Optimization: Another Agile framework, Kanban, focuses on visualizing work and limiting work in progress (WIP) to improve flow and prevent bottlenecks. A Kanban board helps teams track tasks as they move through different stages of development. Continuous improvement in Kanban involves optimizing the flow of work and identifying any areas where tasks get stuck or delayed. By managing WIP limits and continuously improving flow, teams can deliver features faster and more efficiently.

iii. Test-Driven Development (TDD): Test-driven development is a software development approach where tests are written before the code itself. This ensures that the code meets the desired requirements from the start. TDD promotes continuous improvement by reducing the number of bugs that escape production and helping developers write cleaner, more maintainable code. It also encourages frequent refactoring, a practice that improves code quality and long-term maintainability.

iv. Automation and Continuous Integration/Continuous Deployment (CI/CD): Automation plays a critical role in increasing efficiency in iterative development. Automated testing ensures that the code is tested for errors after every change, providing rapid feedback to developers. Similarly, continuous integration and continuous deployment (CI/CD) pipelines automate the process of integrating code changes and deploying them to production, reducing manual errors and speeding up the delivery process. Continuous improvement in CI/CD involves constantly refining the pipeline to make the integration and deployment process faster and more reliable.

BENEFITS OF EFFICIENCY THROUGH ITERATIVE DEVELOPMENT AND CONTINUOUS IMPROVEMENT.

i. Faster Time to Market: By delivering small, functional pieces of software in each sprint, teams can release features to users faster. This "speed to market" advantage enables businesses to respond more quickly to customer needs, seize market opportunities, and stay ahead of competitors.

ii. Higher Quality: Iterative development coupled with continuous improvement leads to higher quality software. By getting early feedback and catching errors sooner, teams can prevent costly rework later. Continuous improvement practices, like refactoring and TDD, help maintain code quality over time, reducing technical debt.

iii. Better Alignment with Business Goals: Agile's focus on customer collaboration and responding to change ensures that the software being developed aligns with evolving business goals. Teams prioritize work that delivers the most value to users and adjust their direction as necessary, ensuring that development efforts are always in sync with the company's objectives.

iv. Improved Team Morale: Continuous improvement fosters a positive team culture, where members are encouraged to share ideas, learn from mistakes, and celebrate successes. This collaborative, adaptive environment boosts morale and empowers teams to feel more ownership and pride in their work.

CHAPTER 3

INCORPORATING DEVOPS FOR CONTINOUS INNOVATION

WHAT IS DEVOPS?

DevOps is a set of practices, philosophies, and tools that integrates development and IT operations, with the aim of improving collaboration and productivity by automating workflows, enhancing communication, and implementing continuous feedback loops. At its core, DevOps focuses on removing the barriers between traditionally sold teams, encouraging shared responsibility for the software from development through to production.

THE KEY PRINCIPLES OF DEVOPS ARE:

i. Collaboration and Communication: DevOps fosters a culture where developers and operations work together closely, with shared goals and responsibilities, resulting in smoother, more aligned workflows.

ii. Automation: By automating repetitive tasks such as testing, integration, deployment, DevOps reduces human error, increases consistency, and speeds up the software delivery process.

iii. Continuous Integration and Continuous Delivery (CI/CD):

DevOps emphasizes the practice of continuously integrating code changes, testing them automatically, and delivering them to production quickly and safely.

Monitoring and Feedback Loops: Continuous monitoring of applications in production environments allows for rapid detection of issues and feedback, which can be quickly addressed, ensuring improved quality over time.

These principles enable software to be developed, tested, and deployed in shorter, more frequent cycles, leading to faster releases and higher-quality software.

Incorporating DevOps into Agile software development is a transformative step that enables businesses to achieve continuous innovation. While Agile emphasizes iterative development and collaboration, DevOps focuses on automating and optimizing the processes between software development and IT operations. Together, these practices create a culture and environment where software can be delivered faster, more reliably, and with improved quality. The convergence of Agile and DevOps fosters a seamless workflow that supports continuous integration, continuous delivery (CI/CD), and ultimately, continuous innovation.

THE DEVOPS PHILOSOPHY

DevOps (short for Development and Operations) is more than just a set of tools—it's a cultural shift that encourages collaboration between development and operations teams. Traditionally, these teams worked in silos, which often led to miscommunication, delays, and bottlenecks in software delivery. DevOps breaks down these silos by fostering a culture of collaboration, shared responsibility, and automation.

THE CORE GOALS OF DEVOPS INCLUDE:

Increased Speed and Agility: DevOps enables organizations to respond quickly to market demands and user feedback by shortening development cycles and delivering new features faster.

Improved Quality and Reliability: Through automation of testing, deployment, and infrastructure management, DevOps reduces human error and improves the consistency and reliability of software.

Scalability and Flexibility: By adopting DevOps, teams can scale applications easily and adjust to changes in demand without compromising on stability or performance.

By integrating development and operations, DevOps bridges the gap between software creation and deployment, promoting a culture of continuous improvement.

The evolution of software development practices over the last two decades has been shaped by a growing need for faster delivery, higher quality, and better collaboration between traditionally separate teams. The rise of

DevOps in modern software development represents a pivotal moment in addressing these needs by blending development (Dev) and operations (Ops) into a unified, collaborative process. This shift has radically transformed the way software is built, tested, deployed, and maintained, allowing organizations to meet the demands of today's fast-paced, innovation-driven digital economy.

HISTORICAL CONTEXT: THE CHALLENGES OF TRADITIONAL SOFTWARE DEVELOPMENT

Before the advent of DevOps, software development teams and IT operations teams worked in silos. Developers would build the software, focusing primarily on functionality and innovation, and then hand it off to operations teams, who were responsible for deploying and maintaining it in production environments. This separation often led to:

i. Delayed Releases: Developers and operations teams worked on different timelines. Developers focused on feature development, while operations teams prioritized stability, leading to delays in deployment as each team had its own goals and processes.

ii. Communication Breakdowns: The lack of collaboration between development and operations resulted in poor communication, with each team unaware of the other's priorities, requirements, and challenges.

iii. Frequent Failures in Production: Developers typically worked in isolated environments that didn't mimic production conditions. This caused issues during deployment, as code that worked in the development environment would often fail in production.

iv. Difficulty in Scaling: Traditional processes were not built for scalability. As the demand for faster delivery of new features grew, these fragmented workflows led to inefficient scaling, both in terms of technology and human resources.

The gap between development and operations created inefficiencies, limited agility, and increased the likelihood of system failures, frustrating both teams and end-users alike. The industry needed a solution that could align the goals of both teams, speed up delivery, and improve reliability—this need gave rise to DevOps.

THE EMERGENCE OF DEVOPS: DRIVING FORCES

The rise of DevOps has been driven by several factors that have shaped modern software development:

a. Agile Methodology: Agile methodologies laid the groundwork for DevOps by emphasizing iterative development, collaboration, and adaptability to changing requirements. However, while Agile improved the development process, it didn't fully address the disconnect between developers and operations. DevOps extended Agile's principles to include operational aspects, ensuring that the entire development lifecycle was streamlined.

b. Cloud Computing: The widespread adoption of cloud computing has been a significant catalyst for the growth of DevOps. Cloud platforms like AWS, Microsoft Azure, and Google Cloud have allowed development and operations teams to work together more efficiently, enabling faster deployment, scalability, and resource management. With the cloud, infrastructure can be treated as code, enabling DevOps practices such as Infrastructure as Code (IaC), where infrastructure can be automated, version-controlled, and replicated easily across environments.

c. Increasing Demand for Faster Software Delivery: In today's digital landscape, businesses are under pressure to deliver software updates, new features, and security patches more rapidly than ever before. DevOps helps organizations meet this demand by automating workflows, reducing bottlenecks, and improving the speed of delivery. Companies that successfully adopt DevOps practices can push updates to production multiple times a day, a necessity in industries where agility and customer responsiveness are critical.

d. Microservices Architecture: The shift towards microservices architecture, where applications are built as a collection of small, loosely coupled services, has further fueled the rise of DevOps. In this model, each service can be developed, deployed, and scaled independently, which aligns well with the principles of DevOps. DevOps practices such as CI/CD and containerization (using Docker or Kubernetes) support the rapid, independent deployment and scaling of these microservices, allowing for continuous innovation.

HOW DEVOPS IMPACTS MODERN SOFTWARE DEVELOPMENT

DevOps has had a profound impact on modern software development in several keyways:

i. Speed and Agility: DevOps allows teams to move faster by automating manual processes and eliminating delays caused by handoffs between development and operations teams. With CI/CD pipelines, code changes can be integrated, tested, and deployed to production much more rapidly, enabling organizations to respond to market demands, customer feedback, and security vulnerabilities in real-time.

ii. Improved Collaboration: DevOps promotes a culture of shared ownership, where developers and operations work together throughout the software lifecycle. This collaboration reduces misunderstandings, speeds up issue resolution, and creates a more cohesive, efficient workflow.

iii. Enhanced Reliability and Stability: With automated testing, monitoring, and continuous deployment, DevOps reduces the risk of errors in production and improves the overall stability of the software. Teams can detect issues early, fix them quickly, and release reliable updates without causing downtime or disruption to users.

iv. Scalability and Flexibility: DevOps practices such as Infrastructure as Code (IaC) and containerization enable teams to scale applications and infrastructure rapidly, without manual intervention. This scalability is essential in today's dynamic cloud environments, where resources need to be allocated efficiently and flexibly to meet changing demands.

v. Continuous Innovation: DevOps creates a feedback loop between development, operations, and users, allowing teams to continuously iterate and improve the software. As a result, organizations can innovate faster, releasing new features and enhancements more frequently, keeping pace with customer expectations and competitive pressures.

TOOLS AND TECHNOLOGIES FUELING DEVOPS GROWTH

The rise of DevOps has been accelerated by the development of various tools and technologies that support its practices. Some key tools include:

i. Version Control (e.g., Git): Allows teams to manage code changes collaboratively, with features for branching, merging, and version tracking.

ii. CI/CD Pipelines (e.g., Jenkins, CircleCI, Travis CI): Automate the process of integrating and testing code changes, enabling continuous deployment.

iii. Containerization (e.g., Docker): Containers allow applications to run consistently across different environments, making deployment and scaling easier.

iv. Orchestration (e.g., Kubernetes): Orchestrates the deployment, scaling, and management of containerized applications, ensuring they run efficiently in production environments.

v. Monitoring and Logging (e.g., Prometheus, ELK Stack, Splunk): These tools provide real-time monitoring, log analysis, and alerting to ensure the reliability and performance of applications in production.

THE FUTURE OF DEVOPS IN SOFTWARE DEVELOPMENT

As software development continues to evolve, the role of DevOps is expected to grow even more significantly. Key trends shaping the future of DevOps include:

a. AI and Machine Learning: The integration of AI into DevOps workflows will help automate even more complex tasks, such as predicting failures and optimizing performance. AI-driven automation can also help improve decision-making by analyzing large sets of operational data.

b. DevSecOps: Security will become a core part of the DevOps process. DevSecOps integrates security practices directly into the CI/CD pipeline, ensuring that security vulnerabilities are detected and addressed early in the development lifecycle.

c. Edge Computing: As edge computing becomes more prevalent, DevOps practices will need to adapt to manage and deploy applications across distributed, decentralized environments.

The rise of DevOps in modern software development represents a paradigm shift that has redefined how teams collaborate, deliver, and innovate. By fostering a culture of automation, shared responsibility, and continuous feedback, DevOps enables organizations to build and deploy software faster, more reliably, and at a scale that meets the demands of today's digital economy. As businesses continue to embrace digital transformation, DevOps will remain a cornerstone of modern software development, driving continuous innovation and operational excellence.

CHAPTER 4

SCALING SOFTWARE DEVELOPMENT THROUGH MICROSERVICES ARCHITECTURE

INTRODUCTION TO MICROSERVICES ARCHITECTURE

Microservices architecture is a modern software design approach where large applications are broken down into smaller, loosely coupled, and independently deployable services. Each microservice focuses on a specific business function, like user authentication, payment processing, or product catalog management. These services interact with each other through APIs, typically using REST or message queues.

The main advantage of microservices is their modularity, which allows developers to build, test, and deploy services independently without affecting the entire system. This leads to faster development cycles, better scalability, and easier maintenance. Since each service can be developed using different technologies, it also offers flexibility in choosing the best tools for each task.

Microservices also enhance fault isolation. If one service fails, it doesn't necessarily bring down the entire application, unlike in monolithic architectures where a single point of failure could impact the whole system. This makes microservices especially well-suited for cloud environments, where horizontal scaling and resilience are critical.

However, microservices come with challenges such as managing the complexity of distributed systems, handling inter-service communication, and ensuring consistency across the various services. Tools like Kubernetes and Docker help manage these complexities by automating the deployment, scaling, and operation of containerized applications.

BENEFITS OF MODULARITY AND SCALABILITY IN SOFTWARE DESIGN

Modularity and scalability in software design offer significant advantages, particularly for large and complex systems:

BENEFITS OF MODULARITY:

i. Easier Maintenance: Since the system is broken into distinct modules, developers can fix bugs, update features, or modify specific parts of the software without affecting the entire application.

ii. Reusability: Modular components can be reused across different parts of an application or even across different projects, reducing duplication of effort and speeding up development.

iii. Parallel Development: Teams can work simultaneously on different modules, enhancing productivity and reducing development time. This is especially useful in larger projects with multiple teams.

iv. Flexibility: Each module can be developed and updated independently, making it easier to adapt to changes in business requirements or technology without overhauling the entire system.

v. Improved Testing: Testing becomes easier because each module can be tested in isolation, leading to quicker identification and resolution of bugs.

BENEFITS OF SCALABILITY:

i. Improved Performance: Scalability allows a system to handle increased workloads by adding resources like processing power, storage, or network capacity. This ensures that applications can maintain performance even as user demand grows.

ii. Cost Efficiency: With scalable design, resources can be allocated dynamically based on demand, allowing businesses to optimize costs by paying for additional resources only when needed.

iii. Futureproofing: Scalable systems are easier to grow and evolve. As the business expands or user base increases, the system can scale up (or down) without requiring a complete redesign or infrastructure overhaul.

iv. Fault Tolerance: Scalable systems can be designed to distribute workloads across multiple instances, reducing the risk of single points of failure. This contributes to higher availability and resilience.

v. Flexibility in Technology Stack: Scalability allows for the integration of different technologies and architectures over time, enabling gradual upgrades or migrations without disrupting the entire system.

ADAPTING LEGACY SYSTEMS TO MICROSERVICES ARCHITECTURE

Adapting legacy systems to a microservices architecture is a complex but highly beneficial process that allows organizations to modernize their software and enhance scalability, flexibility, and efficiency. The transition from monolithic legacy systems to microservices requires careful planning, as it involves breaking down a large, tightly coupled application into independent, manageable services. Here are the key steps and considerations in this transformation:

A. KEY STEPS IN ADAPTING LEGACY SYSTEMS TO MICROSERVICES:

Assess the Existing System: Evaluate the Monolith: Analyze the legacy system's architecture, identifying tightly coupled components and potential boundaries for separation. Understand the system's functionality, interdependence, and critical business processes.

Identify Bottlenecks: Pinpoint performance bottlenecks, areas difficult to maintain, or features that need to be scaled independently. These areas can be good candidates for transitioning to microservices first.

B. DEFINE MICROSERVICE BOUNDARIES:

Decompose the Monolith: Identify logical boundaries within the legacy application, such as business domains or services (e.g., payment, user management, product catalog), and group functionalities into potential microservices.

Domain-Driven Design (DDD): Apply DDD principles to separate the system into bounded contexts that represent distinct microservices.

C. PRIORITIZE INCREMENTAL TRANSITION:

Strangle Pattern: Use the strangler fig pattern to slowly replace parts of the legacy system with microservices. Rather than rewriting everything at once, start by building new features as microservices while leaving the rest of the monolith intact. Over time, refactor or retire legacy components.

API Gateways: Introduce an API gateway to manage interactions between users and both the legacy system and new microservices. This provides a seamless experience during the transition phase.

D. BUILD AND INTEGRATE MICROSERVICES:

Independent Development: Develop each microservice independently, ensuring each one performs a specific function, has its own database (or data store), and communicates with other services through well-defined APIs.

Service-Oriented Interfaces: Implement inter-service communication protocols, like RESTful APIs, message queues (e.g., RabbitMQ, Kafka), or gRPC to enable interaction between microservices.

E. DECOUPLE DATA AND STATE:

Database Separation: Legacy systems typically use a single, large database. For microservices, each service should ideally have its own data store. This avoids tightly coupling services and ensures each can scale independently.

Data Migration Strategy: Plan how to migrate data from the monolithic database to service-specific databases. Use techniques like database replication or event sourcing to keep data in sync during the transition.

F. IMPLEMENT DEVOPS AND CI/CD:

Automated Deployment Pipelines: Build a DevOps pipeline to manage continuous integration (CI) and continuous deployment (CD) of microservices. Tools like Jenkins, GitLab CI, or CircleCI can help automate testing and deployment.

Containerization and Orchestration: Use containers (e.g., Docker) to pack microservices and orchestration tools like Kubernetes to manage scaling, load balancing, and service discovery.

G. MONITOR AND SECURE MICROSERVICES:

Logging and Monitoring: Microservices introduce complexity, so robust logging, monitoring, and alerting are essential. Tools like Prometheus, Grafana, or ELK (Elasticsearch, Logstash, Kibana) can help track service health, performance, and errors.

Security Best Practices: Secure microservices with proper authentication and authorization mechanisms, such as OAuth2 or JWT tokens, and ensure secure communication between services.

Challenges to Consider:

i. Cultural and Organizational Changes: Teams need to embrace a shift from centralized development to more autonomous teams responsible for different microservices. This may require changes in how teams collaborate and manage services.

ii. Data Consistency and Transactions: Managing data consistency across microservices can be challenging, especially when services rely on their own databases. Techniques like eventual consistency or the saga pattern can be used to handle distributed transactions.

iii. Complexity of Distributed Systems: Microservices introduce challenges related to network latency, service coordination, and fault tolerance. Careful attention must be paid to error handling, retries, and fallbacks.

iv. Operational Overhead: While microservices improve scalability and flexibility, they also introduce operational complexities like managing multiple deployments, service monitoring, and debugging in a distributed environment.

BENEFITS OF ADAPTING TO MICROSERVICES:

a. Improved Scalability: Each microservice can scale independently, allowing resources to be allocated more efficiently based on specific needs.

b. Increased Agility: Microservices enable faster and more frequent releases, as each service can be updated and deployed without affecting the entire system.

c. Better Fault Isolation: Issues in one service don't necessarily affect others, improving system stability and uptime.

d. Technology Flexibility: Different microservices can be built using different technologies, frameworks, or programming languages, allowing teams to choose the best tools for each task.

Adapting legacy systems to microservices architecture is a gradual process but can significantly enhance a system's performance, maintainability, and ability to evolve with business needs.

EMBRACING EMERGING TECHNOLOGIES FOR INNOVATION

"Embracing Emerging Technologies for Innovation" is a powerful theme that can be explored across various fields, especially in business, education, and technology. It highlights the importance of leveraging new advancements to drive creativity, enhance efficiency, and solve complex problems.

Here's how this concept can be broken down:

i. Digital Transformation: Embracing technologies such as AI, blockchain, cloud computing, and the Internet of Things (IoT) is essential for organizations seeking to innovate and remain competitive. These tools enable faster decision-making, streamline processes, and offer new opportunities for value creation.

ii. Innovation and Flexibility: New technologies allow businesses to be more flexible and responsive to market changes. For example, AI can predict trends, enabling companies to adapt swiftly. Platforms like Flexibiz would thrive by integrating such technologies, allowing entrepreneurs to innovate and operate efficiently.

iii. Sustainability through Technology: Innovation driven by technology often leads to more sustainable solutions, whether through energy-efficient products or processes that reduce waste. Emerging technologies can help businesses reduce their environmental footprint while enhancing profitability.

iv. Upskilling and Talent Development: As emerging technologies evolve, the demand for new skills grows. Organizations and individuals must continuously learn and adapt to remain relevant, which makes investing in training and development crucial.

How do you plan to incorporate these themes into your work with Flexibiz? Would you like to help crafting content or giving a speech around this idea?

ARTIFICIAL INTELLIGENCE (AI) IN SOFTWARE DEVELOPMENT

Artificial Intelligence (AI) is revolutionizing software development by automating tasks, enhancing productivity, and enabling more innovative solutions. Here are keyways AI transforming the software development landscape:

a. Automated Code Generation

AI tools can assist developers by writing code snippets or even entire programs. Machine learning models, like GitHub's Copilot, help suggest code based on a developer's input, saving time and reducing errors.

b. Bug Detection and Quality Assurance

AI-powered tools can identify bugs in code more quickly and accurately than traditional methods. AI can analyze vast amounts of code to find patterns that often lead to errors, ensuring more reliable software. Tools like DeepCode and Codota enhance code quality by providing real-time recommendations.

c. AI-Driven Testing

Automated testing tools driven by AI can simulate various scenarios, track changes, and test different parts of the software faster than manual methods. This results in more thorough and efficient testing processes, reducing the time-to-market.

d. Natural Language Processing (NLP) for Better User Interaction

NLP enables software to understand and process human language, leading to better chatbots, virtual assistants, and voice-controlled applications. This integration allows software to interact with users more naturally.

e. Predictive Analytics in Project Management

AI can analyze data from past projects to predict project outcomes, estimate delivery timelines, and allocate resources more effectively. This helps project managers in making data-driven decisions and avoiding costly delays.

f. Custom Software Solutions

AI is enabling the development of more personalized software solutions by analyzing user behavior and preferences. This leads to products that are better suited to the needs of specific industries or individuals.

g. AI in Cybersecurity

Incorporating AI into software development helps identify vulnerabilities and protect applications from cyber threats. AI algorithms can detect unusual patterns or anomalies in real time, ensuring better security.

As AI continues to evolve, its role in software development will only grow, making processes more efficient, secure, and innovative. How do you see Flexibiz incorporating AI to enhance its offerings?

INTEGRATING BLOCKCHAIN TECHNOLOGY FOR SECURE AND EFFICIENT APPLICATIONS

Integrating blockchain technology into applications offers several advantages, including security, transparency, and efficiency. Here's how blockchain can enhance your projects:

Data Security: Blockchain uses cryptographic techniques to secure data, ensuring that all transactions or data entries are tamper-resistant and immutable. This can be vital for sectors like finance, healthcare, or logistics.

Transparency: Every transaction recorded on a blockchain is visible to all participants, creating a transparent system where stakeholders can verify data in real time. This increases trust and reduces fraud.

Efficiency and Automation: Smart contracts—self-executing contracts on the blockchain—can automate processes, reducing the need for intermediaries. This streamlines operations, saving time and cost in areas like payments, supply chain management, and identity verification.

Decentralization: Blockchain's decentralized nature eliminates the need for a central authority, reducing single points of failure and providing resilience to attacks.

USING MACHINE LEARNING TO ENHANCE SOFTWARE CAPABILITIES

Integrating machine learning (ML) into software can significantly enhance its capabilities by enabling the system to learn from data, make predictions, and improve over time without explicit programming. Here are some ways ML can be applied to boost software functionalities:

Predictive Analytics: ML algorithms can analyze large datasets to predict trends, outcomes, and behaviors. For example, in business applications, this can help forecast sales, identify market trends, or predict customer churn.

Automation: Machine learning can automate repetitive and complex tasks. For instance, ML can streamline processes like fraud detection, inventory management, or data categorization, making your software more efficient and responsive.

Personalization: ML can create personalized user experiences by analyzing user behavior and preferences. This can be particularly useful on platforms like Flexibiz, where the software could recommend business strategies or tools based on user data.

Natural Language Processing (NLP): If your software involves customer interaction, ML models like NLP can enhance capabilities in understanding and processing human language, enabling better chatbots, automated customer service, or sentiment analysis.

Improved Decision-Making: ML models can help software make data-driven decisions by analyzing past data patterns. This can lead to more accurate predictions in fields like finance, healthcare, or supply chain management.

CHAPTER 5

EMBRACING EMERGING TECHNOLOGIES FOR INNOVATION

Embracing Emerging Technologies for Innovation" is a powerful theme that can be explored across various fields, especially in business, education, and technology. It highlights the importance of leveraging new advancements to drive creativity, enhance efficiency, and solve complex problems.

Here's how this concept can be broken down:

i. Digital Transformation: Embracing technologies such as AI, blockchain, cloud computing, and the Internet of Things (IoT) is essential for organizations seeking to innovate and remain competitive. These tools enable faster decision-making, streamline processes, and offer new opportunities for value creation.

ii. Innovation and Flexibility: New technologies allow businesses to be more flexible and responsive to market changes. For example, AI can predict trends, enabling companies to adapt swiftly. Platforms like Flexibiz would thrive by integrating such technologies, allowing entrepreneurs to innovate and operate efficiently.

iii. Sustainability through Technology: Innovation driven by technology often leads to more sustainable solutions, whether through energy-efficient products or processes that reduce waste. Emerging technologies can help businesses reduce their environmental footprint while enhancing profitability.

iv. Upskilling and Talent Development: As emerging technologies evolve, the demand for new skills grows. Organizations and individuals must continuously learn and adapt to remain relevant, which makes investing in training and development crucial.

How do you plan to incorporate these themes into your work with Flexibiz? Would you like to help crafting content or giving a speech around this idea?

ARTIFICIAL INTELLIGENCE (AI) IN SOFTWARE DEVELOPMENT

Artificial Intelligence (AI) is revolutionizing software development by automating tasks, enhancing productivity, and enabling more innovative solutions. Here are keyways AI transforming the software development landscape:

a. Automated Code Generation

AI tools can assist developers by writing code snippets or even entire programs. Machine learning models, like GitHub's Copilot, help suggest code based on a developer's input, saving time and reducing errors.

b. Bug Detection and Quality Assurance

AI-powered tools can identify bugs in code more quickly and accurately than traditional methods. AI can analyze vast amounts of code to find patterns that often lead to errors, ensuring more reliable software. Tools like DeepCode and Codota enhance code quality by providing real-time recommendations.

c. AI-Driven Testing

Automated testing tools driven by AI can simulate various scenarios, track changes, and test different parts of the software faster than manual methods. This results in more thorough and efficient testing processes, reducing the time-to-market.

d. Natural Language Processing (NLP) for Better User Interaction

NLP enables software to understand and process human language, leading to better chatbots, virtual assistants, and voice-controlled applications. This integration allows software to interact with users more naturally.

e. Predictive Analytics in Project Management

AI can analyze data from past projects to predict project outcomes, estimate delivery timelines, and allocate resources more effectively. This helps project managers in making data-driven decisions and avoiding costly delays.

f. Custom Software Solutions

AI is enabling the development of more personalized software solutions by analyzing user behavior and preferences. This leads to products that are better suited to the needs of specific industries or individuals.

g. AI in Cybersecurity

Incorporating AI into software development helps identify vulnerabilities and protect applications from cyber threats. AI algorithms can detect unusual patterns or anomalies in real time, ensuring better security.

As AI continues to evolve, its role in software development will only grow, making processes more efficient, secure, and innovative. How do you see Flexibiz incorporating AI to enhance its offerings?

INTEGRATING BLOCKCHAIN TECHNOLOGY FOR SECURE AND EFFICIENT APPLICATIONS

Integrating blockchain technology into applications offers several advantages, including security, transparency, and efficiency. Here's how blockchain can enhance your projects:

Data Security: Blockchain uses cryptographic techniques to secure data, ensuring that all transactions or data entries are tamper-resistant and immutable. This can be vital for sectors like finance, healthcare, or logistics.

Transparency: Every transaction recorded on a blockchain is visible to all participants, creating a transparent system where stakeholders can verify data in real time. This increases trust and reduces fraud.

Efficiency and Automation: Smart contracts—self-executing contracts on the blockchain—can automate processes, reducing the need for intermediaries. This streamlines operations, saving time and cost in areas like payments, supply chain management, and identity verification.

Decentralization: Blockchain's decentralized nature eliminates the need for a central authority, reducing single points of failure and providing resilience to attacks.

USING MACHINE LEARNING TO ENHANCE SOFTWARE CAPABILITIES

Integrating machine learning (ML) into software can significantly enhance its capabilities by enabling the system to learn from data, make predictions, and improve over time without explicit programming. Here are some ways ML can be applied to boost software functionalities:

Predictive Analytics: ML algorithms can analyze large datasets to predict trends, outcomes, and behaviors. For example, in business applications, this can help forecast sales, identify market trends, or predict customer churn.

Automation: Machine learning can automate repetitive and complex tasks. For instance, ML can streamline processes like fraud detection, inventory management, or data categorization, making your software more efficient and responsive.

Personalization: ML can create personalized user experiences by analyzing user behavior and preferences. This can be particularly useful on platforms like Flexibiz, where the software could recommend business strategies or tools based on user data.

Natural Language Processing (NLP): If your software involves customer interaction, ML models like NLP can enhance capabilities in understanding and processing human language, enabling better chatbots, automated customer service, or sentiment analysis.

Improved Decision-Making: ML models can help software make data-driven decisions by analyzing past data patterns. This can lead to more accurate predictions in fields like finance, healthcare, or supply chain management.

CHAPTER 6

EFFECTIVE TEAM COLLABORATIONS AND COMMUNICATIONS

Effective collaboration and communication are essential for the success of any team, especially in fast-paced industries like software development, business operations, and creative projects. When teams communicate well and work together efficiently, they can achieve higher levels of productivity, innovation, and job satisfaction.

A. THE IMPORTANCE OF COLLABORATION IN TEAMS

Collaboration refers to team members working together toward a common goal, combining their individual skills, knowledge, and experience. Key benefits include:

Increased innovation: Different perspectives often lead to more creative problem-solving and innovative ideas.

Improved efficiency: Collaborative teams can distribute tasks based on individual strengths, ensuring that work is completed faster and more accurately.

Stronger relationships: Working together fosters trust, respect, and mutual support, leading to better team dynamics.

Better problem-solving: With input from multiple team members, solutions to challenges can be more robust and holistic.

B. BUILDING A CULTURE OF COLLABORATION

Creating a collaborative environment starts with company culture. Leaders and team members should prioritize:

Open communication: Encourage team members to share ideas, ask questions, and provide feedback without fear of criticism.

Defined roles: Ensure everyone understands their responsibilities and how their work fits into the larger project.

Shared goals: Align team efforts around common objectives and provide clear guidance on how each member's contribution supports those goals.

Recognition and support: Celebrate collaborative successes and provide support for team members facing challenges, fostering a sense of belonging and teamwork.

C. EFFECTIVE COMMUNICATION STRATEGIES

Clear communication is the backbone of successful collaboration. Here are key strategies to enhance communication within teams:

Active listening: Encourage team members to listen attentively to each other, ask clarifying questions, and avoid interrupting. This ensures that everyone feels heard and valued.

Clarity and brevity: Promote clear and concise communication to avoid misunderstandings. Whether in meetings, emails, or chats, team members should focus on the key message.

Constructive feedback: Create a culture where feedback is given in a constructive and positive manner. Feedback should focus on finding solutions and improving performance, rather than on assigning blame.

Non-verbal communication: In video calls or face-to-face interactions, body language, facial expressions, and tone of voice play an important role in how messages are perceived. Team members should be mindful of how they present themselves.

D. TOOLS FOR ENHANCING COLLABORATION AND COMMUNICATION

The right tools can enhance team collaboration and streamline communication. Here are some popular tools:

Slack: A real-time messaging platform that helps teams communicate efficiently through dedicated channels for different projects or topics.

Microsoft Teams: Offers messaging, video conferencing, and file-sharing capabilities in one platform, making it easy for teams to collaborate in real-time.

Google Workspace: Tools like Google Docs, Sheets, and Slides allow teams to collaborate on documents, presentations, and spreadsheets in real time, regardless of location.

Asana/Trello: Project management tools that help teams track tasks, deadlines, and project progress in a visual, user-friendly way.

Zoom: A video conferencing tool that supports virtual meetings, team discussions, and webinars, especially for remote teams.

E. ENCOURAGING CROSS-FUNCTIONAL COLLABORATION

Cross-functional teams consist of members with different expertise working toward a common goal. Encouraging collaboration between different functions (e.g., marketing, design, development) helps ensure:

Holistic problem-solving: Each team member brings a unique perspective to the table, leading to more comprehensive solutions.

Greater alignment with business objectives: Including members from various departments ensures that the team's work aligns with overall business goals, user needs, and market trends.

Reduced bottlenecks: Cross-functional teams help streamline communication and decision-making, as all key players are involved from the outset.

F. HANDLING CONFLICT IN TEAMS

Conflict is inevitable in any team, but how it is handled can either improve or damage team collaboration. To manage conflict effectively:

Address conflicts early: Encourage open discussions about issues as soon as they arise to prevent them from escalating.

Focus on solutions: During conflicts, steer the conversation toward finding solutions that are acceptable to all parties involved.

Use mediation when needed: If conflicts can't be resolved internally, consider bringing in a neutral third party to mediate and find common ground.

G. LEADERSHIP'S ROLE IN FOSTERING COLLABORATION

Leaders play a crucial role in shaping how teams collaborate. Effective leaders

Lead by example, show collaborative behavior by encouraging input from all team members, being transparent, and engaging in open communication.

Empower the team: Give team members the autonomy to make decisions and take ownership of their work, promoting accountability and responsibility.

Provide resources: Ensure the team has access to the necessary tools and training to collaborate effectively.

Build trust: Trust is key to collaboration. Leaders should foster a culture of trust by being reliable, honest, and supportive.

THE IMPORTANCE OF CROSS-FUNCTIONAL TEAMS IN SOFTWARE DEVELOPMENT

Cross-functional teams play a critical role in software development by bringing together diverse expertise from various departments, such as design, development, testing, and marketing. Here's why they are important:

a. Improved Collaboration and Communication: By involving different functions early in the development process, cross-functional teams foster better communication and understanding across disciplines. This reduces the risk of misaligned goals and ensures that everyone works toward a common objective.

b. Faster Problem Solving: With multiple perspectives in the same room, problems can be identified and addressed more quickly. Developers, designers, and marketers can collaborate to find solutions that are technically feasible, user-friendly, and market ready.

b. Increased Innovation: Cross-functional teams combine a variety of skills and insights, encouraging creativity and innovation. This blend of knowledge leads to more robust and creative solutions that a single-discipline team might overlook.

d. Greater Accountability: In a cross-functional setup, team members from different departments feel equally responsible for the project's success. This shared ownership improves accountability and ensures all aspects of the product are developed with equal attention.

c. Faster Time-to-Market: With all relevant functions working together simultaneously, cross-functional teams can significantly reduce the time-to-market. Collaboration accelerates decision-making and prevents delays caused by sequential hand-offs between departments.

d. Enhanced Product Quality: Cross-functional teams ensure that all aspects of the product—whether technical, design, or customer-focused—are well-considered throughout the development lifecycle, leading to higher quality outcomes.

In software development, adopting cross-functional teams is an effective way to create more cohesive, innovative, and high-quality products.

TOOLS AND PLATFORMS THAT ENHANCE COLLABORATION AND PRODUCTIVITY

There are many tools and platforms designed to enhance collaboration and productivity, especially in cross-functional teams. These tools help streamline communication, project management, and overall efficiency. Here are some key categories and examples:

PROJECT MANAGEMENT TOOLS

These platforms help teams organize tasks, assign responsibilities, track progress, and manage timelines.

Trello: A visual project management tool using boards, lists, and cards to organize tasks.

Asana: Provides task lists, project timelines, and milestones for team members to track the project status.

Jira: Popular among software development teams for managing agile projects, tracking bugs, and monitoring releases.

COMMUNICATION TOOLS

These tools enable real-time collaboration and reduce email overload.

Slack: A messaging platform that facilitates team communication through channels, direct messages, and integration with other tools.

Microsoft Teams: A collaboration platform that combines workplace chat, meetings, and file sharing, with seamless integration into the Microsoft Office suite.

Zoom: A video conferencing tool for virtual meetings, especially for remote teams.

DOCUMENT COLLABORATION TOOLS

These platforms allow multiple users to work on the same documents in real time.

Google Workspace (Docs, Sheets, Slides): Google's suite of cloud-based collaboration tools allows teams to work together on documents, spreadsheets, and presentations in real-time.

Microsoft 365 (Word, Excel, PowerPoint): Microsoft's cloud-based office suite integrates with Teams, enabling real-time co-authoring and sharing.

Notion: Combines notetaking, document creation, and task management for collaborative team spaces.

VERSION CONTROL AND CODE COLLABORATION TOOLS

These are essential for software development teams to collaborate on code.

GitHub: A platform for version control and code collaboration, allowing developers to work on the same codebase simultaneously, with features like pull requests and issue tracking.

GitLab: Similar to GitHub, GitLab offers built-in CI/CD pipelines for testing and deploying code automatically.

Bitbucket: A code hosting and collaboration tool integrated with Jira for seamless project tracking.

DESIGN AND PROTOTYPING TOOLS

Designers and developers can collaborate on UI/UX prototypes to streamline feedback and revisions.

Figma: A cloud-based design tool that allows real-time collaboration on designs and prototypes.

Sketch: A digital design tool popular among UX/UI designers, with collaboration plugins for real-time feedback.

Invision: A prototyping tool that allows teams to collaborate on design mockups and gather feedback.

FILE SHARING AND CLOUD STORAGE

These platforms facilitate easy file sharing, version control, and remote access to files.

Google Drive: Cloud storage with easy sharing and collaboration on files stored in the cloud.

Dropbox: File-sharing and cloud storage service that allows teams to organize and share large files seamlessly.

OneDrive: Microsoft's cloud storage service, which integrates well with other Office 365 tools for collaboration.

TIME MANAGEMENT AND PRODUCTIVITY TOOLS

These tools help individuals and teams stay on track with their time and productivity.

Toggl: A time-tracking tool that helps teams understand where their time is going, improving productivity.

Rescue Time: Monitors how time is spent on devices and offers insights to optimize productivity.

Todo list: A simple task manager that helps individuals organize their to-do lists and collaborate on shared tasks.

DEVOPS AND CI/CD TOOLS

For software teams, these platforms streamline development, testing, and deployment.

Jenkins: An open-source automation tool that facilitates continuous integration and delivery (CI/CD).

CircleCI: Provides CI/CD pipelines to automate testing and deployment.

Azure DevOps: A set of development tools to support version control, project management, and CI/CD pipelines.

By integrating these tools into their workflow, teams can boost collaboration, streamline communication, manage projects more effectively, and ultimately enhance productivity.

CULTIVATING A CULTURE OF INNOVATION WITHIN DEVELOPMENT TEAMS

Cultivating a culture of innovation within development teams is key to driving continuous improvement, creativity, and long-term success. Here are some strategies to foster this culture:

Encourage Experimentation: Create an environment where team members feel safe to try new things, even if they fail. This means supporting risk-taking and viewing failures as opportunities for learning rather than setbacks.

Cross-functional Collaboration: Encourage teams to work with other departments or disciplines. Diverse perspectives can lead to more creative problem-solving and innovative solutions.

Open Communication: Promote transparent communication channels where everyone can share ideas freely, regardless of hierarchy. Hold regular brainstorming sessions or innovation workshops to give space for new ideas to the surface.

Invest in Learning and Development: Offer access to training, workshops, and conferences to help team members stay up to date with industry trends and cutting-edge technologies. Providing time for personal projects and exploration can also stimulate innovation.

Reward Innovation: Recognize and reward individuals or teams who contribute to innovative ideas or solutions. This can be through formal rewards like bonuses or informal recognition like celebrating achievements in meetings.

Empower Autonomy: Trust your development teams to make decisions about how they approach problems and solutions. Allowing autonomy in how work gets done can drive more creative approaches.

Set Innovation Goals: Establish clear innovation objectives that align with the company's overall vision. This helps direct creative energy towards goals that are meaningful for the organization.

Create a Flexible Environment: Provide tools, flexible workspaces, and schedules that support creative thinking. Whether through remote work, flexible hours, or even relaxed office environments, this can help foster out-of-the-box thinking.

Leverage Technology: Use the latest technology and tools that enhance productivity and collaboration, such as project management software, AI-driven analytics, and cloud-based platforms.

Leadership by Example: Leaders should model innovative behavior, showing a willingness to embrace new technologies and processes. When leaders champion innovation, the rest of the team will follow.

Building such a culture requires consistency and patience but can lead to a dynamic, forward-thinking team that is capable of pushing boundaries and maintaining a competitive edge.

CHAPTER 7

USER-CENTRIC DESIGN AND INNOVATION

User-centric design is a methodology focused on optimizing the user experience (UX) by deeply understanding the users' needs, goals, and pain points. Unlike traditional design processes that prioritize technical capabilities or business goals, user-centric design begins with empathy—seeing the product or service from the perspective of the people who will use it.

KEY PRINCIPLES OF USER-CENTRIC DESIGN:

Empathy: Understanding the emotional and practical needs of the users.

User Feedback: Iterative design cycles that continuously integrate real user feedback.

Simplicity: Avoiding complexity to ensure ease of use.

Accessibility: Designing for inclusivity, making the product usable by the broadest audience possible.

HOW USER-CENTRIC DESIGN DRIVES INNOVATION

When companies deeply understand their users, they are better positioned to innovate in ways that truly matter. By putting user needs at the forefront, development teams can avoid "solution-first" thinking, where technology is built without first confirming that it solves a real problem.

KEYWAYS USER-CENTRIC DESIGN PROMOTES INNOVATION:

Solving Real Problems: Products are created to address genuine user needs, leading to solutions that resonate with the market.

Improving Usability: By focusing on simplicity and user-friendliness, companies can develop more intuitive and accessible solutions that improve the overall user experience.

Enabling Iteration: Continuous feedback from users allows teams to rapidly iterate, improving features, and identifying new opportunities for innovation.

Driving Customer Loyalty: When products are designed to meet real user needs, customers are more likely to stay loyal and advocate for the brand.

CHALLENGES IN IMPLEMENTING USER-CENTRIC DESIGN

While user-centric design offers many benefits, implementing it successfully can be challenging. Common obstacles include:

Limited Resources: Conducting user research and frequent iterations can be resource intensive.

Conflicting Stakeholder Interests: Balancing user needs with business goals may create friction between design teams and leadership.

Data Overload: With a large amount of user feedback, it can be difficult to decide which insights to prioritize.

UNDERSTANDING THE USER EXPERIENCE (UX) AS A DRIVER OF INNOVATION

User experience (UX) refers to how a user interacts with and experiences a product, system, or service. It encompasses all aspects of a user's interaction, including the interface, usability, performance, and even emotional responses. UX design is essential because it impacts customer satisfaction, loyalty, and overall brand perception. When done right, UX becomes a critical driver of innovation.

HERE'S HOW UNDERSTANDING UX CAN DRIVE INNOVATION:

Focusing on User Needs to Inform Innovation

Innovation begins with solving real problems for users. By focusing on the user's needs, preferences, and behaviors, companies can identify pain points and areas of improvement that traditional development methods may overlook. Understanding how users interact with a product can lead to breakthrough innovations that create value where it is most needed.

Example: Airbnb revolutionized the hospitality industry by identifying a need for travelers to find affordable, convenient lodging while allowing hosts to monetize extra space. Their UX innovations, such as an easy-to-use platform and secure communication channels, made the service accessible to a broad audience and redefined how people travel.

Improving Usability and Accessibility

A great user experience simplifies complex processes, making products more accessible and intuitive. This creates opportunities for innovation, especially when a product or service is made easier to use or accessible to a broader range of people, including those with disabilities or less tech-savvy users.

Example: Google's minimalist search interface is an example of UX innovation. By focusing on simplicity, the search engine's design removes distractions and allows users to quickly access the information they need. The company constantly iterates based on user feedback, driving continuous innovation in search technology.

Encouraging Emotional Connection

UX is not just about functionality; it's also about creating an emotional connection with users. Products that evoke positive emotional responses, whether through design, interaction, or messaging—can lead to higher levels of engagement and loyalty. When companies prioritize emotional UX, they create experiences that resonate with users on a deeper level, sparking innovations in design, marketing, and user interaction.

Example: Apple's product ecosystem is known for creating an emotional connection with its users through sleek design, intuitive functionality, and a seamless experience across devices. Apple's focus on UX has consistently driven innovation in personal technology, turning loyal users into brand advocates.

Data-Driven Iteration for Continuous Improvement

Understanding user experience involves gathering data from user interactions, behavior analytics, and direct feedback. This data can fuel continuous improvement and iterative innovation. When teams analyze user data to understand patterns, they can refine products in ways that directly address user needs, leading to more effective innovations.

Example: Netflix continually innovates its platform by leveraging user data to enhance the viewing experience. The platform's recommendation algorithm, driven by user behavior, is an example of data-informed UX innovation that keeps users engaged and returning to the service.

Prototyping and Testing New Ideas

UX design often involves rapid prototyping and testing, which provides teams with the ability to experiment and gather feedback early in the product development cycle. This process fosters innovation by allowing teams to explore multiple solutions to a problem, discard those that don't work, and iterate on those that do.

Example: IDEO, the global design consultancy, is known for using prototyping as part of their design thinking process. By creating early models of their designs and testing them with real users, they've pioneered innovative products across industries, from health care to consumer electronics.

Integrating Feedback Loops for Ongoing Innovation

A user-centric approach to UX involves creating feedback loops where users continuously provide input on their experiences. This feedback serves as a wellspring for new ideas and improvements, ensuring that innovation doesn't stop after a product is launched. By incorporating feedback into the development process, companies ensure that their products evolve to meet changing user expectations.

Example: Slack, a popular team collaboration tool, constantly collects feedback from its users through surveys, user interviews, and community forums. This feedback is directly integrated into product updates, leading to regular innovations that improve functionality, enhance integrations, and streamline the user interface.

Anticipating Future User Needs

To drive innovation through UX, companies must also anticipate the future needs of users. By observing trends, new technologies, and shifts in user behavior, companies can stay ahead of the curve and innovate preemptively. Predictive UX design can help companies adapt to emerging markets and technologies before competitors catch on.

Example: Spotify's shift towards podcasts and personalized playlists anticipated user demand for a more diverse and personalized audio experience. By using data to predict user preferences and emerging trends, Spotify has continued to innovate its platform beyond traditional music streaming.

UX as a Catalyst for Innovation

UX is not just about making products look good or working better, it's about deeply understanding user behavior, needs, and expectations. When companies prioritize UX as a driver of innovation, they create products and services that not only solve problems but do so in ways that are intuitive, engaging, and future focused. UX-driven innovation ensures that companies remain competitive, relevant, and aligned with the evolving needs of their users.

CONDUCTING USER RESEARCH FOR INFORMED DEVELOPMENT DECISIONS

User research is a critical process that helps development teams make informed decisions about product design, functionality, and user experience. It involves gathering qualitative and quantitative insights from real users to understand their needs, behaviors, pain points, and expectations. Conducting thorough user research ensures that product development is aligned with user needs, leading to solutions that are not only innovative but also user-friendly and effective.

Here's how to conduct user research to drive informed development decisions:

a. Defining Research Objectives

Before starting any user research, it's essential to define clear objectives. Understanding what you want to achieve with your research will help you select the right methods and questions. Common objectives might include:

i. Identifying user pain points with current solutions.

ii. Understanding how users interact with similar products.

iii. Gauging user reactions to new features or designs.

iv. Exploring the needs and preferences of a target demographic.

Key questions to ask:

i. What specific problems are we trying to solve?

ii. Who are the key users, and what do we want to learn about their behavior or preferences?

iii. What development decisions will be informed by this research?

b. Choosing the Right Research Methods

Different research methods provide different types of insights. Depending on your objectives, you may want to use a combination of qualitative and quantitative methods.

QUALITATIVE METHODS:

User Interviews: One-on-one conversations that allow you to dive deeply into user behaviors, motivations, and pain points.

Focus Groups: Group discussions that help gather insights on shared user experiences and expectations.

Usability Testing: Observing users as they interact with a product to identify usability issues, confusion, or frustration.

Field Studies: Watching users in their natural environment to see how they use products in real-life scenarios.

QUANTITATIVE METHODS:

Surveys: Gathering numerical data from a large sample of users to identify patterns, preferences, or satisfaction levels.

Analytics and User Data: Using data from tools like Google Analytics, heatmaps, or other tracking software to understand how users interact with digital products.

A/B Testing: Comparing different versions of a product or feature to see which performs better with users.

Example: If your goal is to improve the user interface (UI) of a mobile app, you might start with usability testing to observe how users navigate the current interface. You could then follow up with a survey to gather more structured feedback from a larger user base.

IDENTIFYING AND RECRUITING PARTICIPANTS

To ensure your research yields relevant insights, it's essential to identify and recruit the right participants. Your research should focus on users who closely resemble your target audience.

Key considerations:

Demographics: Age, location, profession, or any characteristics that align with your product's target market.

Behavior: How frequently they use your product or similar solutions, their goals, and pain points.

Recruitment channels: Use email lists, social media, product communities, or third-party services to recruit participants. Offering incentives (e.g., discounts, gift cards) can increase participation.

Example: If you're developing a product for small business owners, recruit participants who own or manage businesses, ensuring they represent the diversity of your target market.

COLLECTING AND ANALYZING DATA

Once your research is underway, the next step is collecting and analyzing the data. It's important to document all findings systematically, whether through notes, audio recordings, videos, or survey responses. The goal is to organize the information in a way that makes patterns, insights, and trends clear.

ANALYZING QUALITATIVE DATA:

Identify Themes: Group feedback into themes or categories, such as common user frustrations, frequently mentioned features, or unexpected behaviors.

Create User Personas: Develop fictional representations of key user types based on the data to help guide development decisions. Personas can reflect a range of user behaviors, needs, and preferences.

ANALYZING QUANTITATIVE DATA:

Statistical Analysis: Use tools like spreadsheets or data analysis software to identify patterns in survey responses, usage data, or A/B test results.

Benchmarking: Compare data points like task completion rates, user satisfaction scores, or bounce rates against industry standards or your own historical data.

Example: After conducting user interviews and surveys, you might discover that users are frustrated with how long it takes to complete tasks on your platform. By analyzing both qualitative feedback and quantitative data (e.g., time spent on tasks), you can pinpoint which areas need optimization.

CREATING ACTIONABLE INSIGHTS

The primary goal of user research is to translate the data into actionable insights that inform development decisions. This is where the research findings are distilled into clear recommendations.

STEPS TO CREATE ACTIONABLE INSIGHTS:

Prioritize Findings: Not all feedback is equally important. Identify the most critical pain points or opportunities for improvement that will have the most significant impact on user experience and business goals.

Present the Data Visually: Use graphs, charts, or visualizations to present quantitative data. For qualitative insights, creating user journey maps can show how users move through a product or system.

Link Insights into Product Development: Connect the research findings directly to development decisions. For example, if users are struggling with navigation, it may lead to redesigning the UI to make it more intuitive.

Example: After discovering that users frequently abandon their shopping carts due to a complex checkout process, the actionable insight might be: "Simplify the checkout process by reducing the number of steps and adding a progress bar."

VALIDATING SOLUTIONS WITH ONGOING RESEARCH

User research is not a one-time event; it should be an ongoing process that informs each phase of product development. Once you've implemented changes based on initial research, it's essential to validate those solutions by conducting follow-up research.

METHODS FOR VALIDATION:

Usability Testing of New Features: Test how users respond to newly implemented changes to ensure they've addressed the identified issues.

Surveys and Feedback Collection: Gather feedback from a broader audience to confirm that the changes are effective.

Continuous Monitoring: Use analytics and user behavior tracking to ensure that the product continues to meet user needs over time.

Example: If you've redesigned a mobile app's navigation based on user feedback, conduct a round of usability testing with the updated design to ensure the changes have resolved the identified issues.

Conducting user research is a powerful tool for making informed development decisions. By understanding your users, their behaviors, and pain points, you can create products that are intuitive, meet real needs, and stand out in the market. Through a structured approach, defining objectives, choosing the right methods, recruiting the right participants, and translating data into actionable insights, you can ensure that user research becomes a key driver of innovation and product success.

HOW USER FEEDBACK LOOPS IMPROVE BOTH INNOVATION AND EFFICIENCY

User feedback loops are essential mechanisms that enable continuous learning, improvement, and adaptation in product development. By regularly collecting, analyzing, and implementing user feedback, businesses can make informed decisions, fostering innovation and enhancing operational efficiency. These feedback loops help organizations stay aligned with customer needs, quickly resolve issues, and identify new opportunities for growth.

Here's how user feedback loops improve both innovation and efficiency:

DRIVING CONTINUOUS INNOVATION THROUGH ITERATION

User feedback loops enable teams to consistently receive input from the people who interact with their product or service. This ongoing stream of insights helps businesses stay responsive to evolving user needs and preferences, allowing them to innovate continuously. The iterative process of testing, gathering feedback, and refining ideas fosters an environment where innovation is ongoing rather than a one-time event.

BENEFITS TO INNOVATION:

Identifying New Opportunities: Direct feedback helps uncover unmet user needs, pain points, or desires, which can spark the development of new features, products, or services.

Testing Hypotheses: Teams can prototype and test new ideas quickly, using feedback to confirm whether a feature solves a real problem before fully investing in its development.

Enhancing Creativity: By involving users in the creative process, teams can gather diverse perspectives, leading to more creative and user-driven innovations.

Example: Slack's approach to innovation involves actively listening to users through feedback loops. By incorporating customer suggestions, they've continuously introduced new features like custom workflows and integrations, which have improved the user experience and differentiated the platform from competitors.

IMPROVING EFFICIENCY THROUGH QUICK PROBLEM RESOLUTION

One of the most immediate benefits of user feedback loops is the ability to quickly identify and address problems. Regular feedback allows teams to catch issues early, reducing the time and resources spent on troubleshooting and minimizing the impact on the user experience.

BENEFITS TO EFFICIENCY:

Early Detection of Issues: Continuous feedback can highlight problems with performance, usability, or functionality before they become widespread, allowing for faster resolution.

Reduced Development Costs: Identifying problems early in the development cycle prevents wasted resources on solutions that don't meet user expectations.

Prioritization of Resources: Feedback loops help teams focus on the most critical issues or feature requests, ensuring that time and resources are used efficiently.

Example: Spotify frequently relies on user feedback to fine-tune its features. For instance, when users pointed out usability issues with playlist management, the company quickly iterated on their UI, resolving the issues and improving the overall experience without major disruptions.

Enhancing Product-Market Fit

User feedback loops are invaluable for ensuring that a product maintains a strong product-market fit. By regularly gathering feedback, companies can confirm that their product continues to align with the needs of its target audience. This process reduces the risk of developing features or products that are out of sync with market demands, ensuring that innovation is both relevant and valuable.

BENEFITS TO INNOVATION:

Alignment with User Needs: Regular feedback ensures that product development is driven by real user needs and preferences, increasing the likelihood that innovations will be adopted and appreciated by the market.

Adaptation to Market Trends: As user preferences evolve, feedback loops help companies stay ahead of trends and pivot quickly if needed, keeping the product competitive.

Example: Airbnb's use of feedback loops helped them expand beyond just short-term rentals to experiences and long-term stays, responding to user demands and shifts in the travel market, especially during the COVID-19 pandemic. This flexibility allowed Airbnb to adapt and maintain relevance during challenging times.

ENABLING DATA-DRIVEN DECISION MAKING

User feedback loops generate valuable data that can be analyzed to inform decision-making processes. This data provides evidence-based insights into user behavior, preferences, and frustrations, enabling development teams to make decisions that are more accurate and aligned with real user needs.

BENEFITS TO EFFICIENCY:

Reduced Guesswork: With data-driven insights, teams spend less time speculating about what users want and can make informed decisions based on actual user behavior.

Faster Development Cycles: Continuous feedback allows teams to validate ideas early, speeding up development cycles by eliminating unnecessary iterations on unproven concepts.

Optimized Resource Allocation: By prioritizing features or fixes based on user feedback, teams can allocate resources more effectively, focusing on high-impact areas.

Example: Netflix continuously collects feedback from user interactions with its platform. This feedback informs us of decisions on content recommendations, interface design, and new features. By making data-driven decisions, Netflix can quickly adapt and optimize the platform for maximum user engagement.

Fostering a Customer-Centric Culture

Regular feedback loops help build a strong connection between the development team and the users they serve. When teams are consistently exposed to user opinions and feedback, they become more customer-focused, which can lead to better decision-making and innovations that truly address user needs.

BENEFITS TO INNOVATION:

Empathy-Driven Solutions: Teams that regularly hear from users can empathize with their challenges, driving the development of solutions that are truly user-centric.

Collaborative Innovation: Engaging users in the product development process encourages a collaborative relationship, where users feel heard and valued. This can lead to co-creation, where users contribute to the innovation process.

Example: Microsoft's shift toward a more customer-centric culture, particularly with their Office 365 and Azure platforms, has been driven by feedback loops. By actively listening to user feedback through forums and community interactions, Microsoft has been able to roll out user-driven updates and improve customer satisfaction significantly.

REDUCING TIME-TO-MARKET

With user feedback integrated throughout the development process, companies can streamline decision-making and prioritize features that provide the most value. This approach reduces the time spent on developing unnecessary features, helping businesses bring new products or updates to the market faster.

BENEFITS TO EFFICIENCY:

Faster Iteration Cycles: Regular feedback allows for faster validation and iteration, leading to quicker development cycles and earlier product launches.

Prioritized Development: Feedback loops help prioritize the most impactful features, ensuring that teams focus on delivering high-value updates without unnecessary delays.

Agility in Response to Market Changes: Continuous feedback allows teams to pivot quickly if user needs or market conditions change, improving overall agility.

Example: Amazon's product development process is highly iterative and customer-focused, relying heavily on user feedback loops. This enables

Amazon to quickly launch new features and services that meet user expectations while minimizing the risk of failure or costly delays.

Building Long-Term Customer Loyalty

By consistently acting on user feedback, companies show customers that they value their input and are dedicated to improving the product based on their needs. This approach builds trust and strengthens customer loyalty, as users feel more invested in the product's success and are more likely to remain long-term users.

BENEFITS TO INNOVATION:

Customer Retention: Acting on feedback fosters loyalty, which can result in higher user retention and advocacy for the product.

Crowdsourced Innovation: Engaging users in feedback loops creates a sense of ownership, encouraging them to contribute more ideas and suggestions, further driving innovation.

Example: Adobe's transition to a subscription-based model with Creative Cloud was guided by extensive user feedback. By continually incorporating user suggestions and improvements, Adobe has maintained high customer satisfaction and loyalty in a highly competitive market.

User feedback loops are powerful tools that simultaneously drive innovation and enhance efficiency. By continuously gathering and acting on user feedback, companies can develop products that better meet user needs, reduce the time and cost of development, and stay ahead of competitors. Whether through early detection of issues, data-driven decision-making, or fostering long-term customer loyalty, feedback loops create a continuous cycle of improvement, resulting in a more innovative, user-focused, and efficient development process.

CHAPTER 8

SECURITY AS A FOUNDATION FOR INNOVATION

In today's digital landscape, security is no longer just a reactive defense mechanism; it has become a critical enabler of innovation. As businesses push the boundaries of technology, from cloud computing to artificial intelligence and the Internet of Things (IoT), maintaining robust security practices ensures that these innovations can thrive in a trusted and safe environment. A strong security foundation protects intellectual property, fosters customer trust, and ensures compliance with regulatory standards, all of which are essential for long-term innovation.

Here's how security serves as a foundation for innovation:

1. BUILDING TRUST FOR INNOVATIVE SOLUTIONS

Security is crucial in building and maintaining trust between businesses and their customers. Users are more likely to adopt new technologies and innovations when they feel confident that their data and privacy are protected. Without trust, even the most advanced innovations may fail to gain widespread acceptance.

BENEFITS TO INNOVATION:

Increased Adoption Rates: Secure products encourage users to adopt new solutions, particularly in industries where privacy and data protection are critical, such as finance, healthcare, and e-commerce.

Customer Loyalty: When users know their data is secure, they are more likely to remain loyal to a brand, even as it introduces new and innovative features.

Reduced Risk of Backlash: Innovating without strong security measures can lead to data breaches or privacy scandals, damaging brand reputation and customer trust.

Example: Apple's focus on privacy and security as core values has made its devices and services more attractive to customers, enabling innovations like Face ID and encrypted messaging services (iMessage) to thrive in an environment where users feel safe using their devices.

2. ENABLING SAFE EXPERIMENTATION

Innovative companies often push the limits of technology, experimenting with new ideas and approaches. However, without a strong security infrastructure, these experiments can expose businesses to risks like data breaches, intellectual property theft, or regulatory fines. Security acts as a safety net, allowing businesses to experiment and innovate without fear of compromising sensitive data or violating regulations.

BENEFITS TO INNOVATION:

Safe Prototyping and Testing: With a secure environment, businesses can test new products and features in a controlled way, ensuring that any vulnerabilities or weaknesses are addressed before a full launch.

Innovation in High-Risk Areas: Security enables innovation in sensitive sectors like fintech, health tech, and autonomous systems, where privacy and safety concerns could otherwise hinder development.

Compliance with Regulations: By integrating security into the innovation process, companies can ensure they meet legal requirements like GDPR, HIPAA, or PCI-DSS, avoiding costly fines or delays.

Example: In the financial services industry, companies like PayPal and Stripe have integrated advanced encryption and fraud detection into their platforms, allowing them to innovate with new payment solutions while ensuring regulatory compliance and protecting customer data.

3. PROTECTING INTELLECTUAL PROPERTY

Innovation often involves the creation of valuable intellectual property (IP), such as proprietary software, algorithms, or designs. Without robust security measures in place, this intellectual property is vulnerable to theft by competitors, hackers, or insiders. Securing IP not only protects the company's competitive edge but also encourages more investment in research and development (R&D).

BENEFITS TO INNOVATION:

Safeguarding R&D Investments: Security ensures that years of research, design, and testing are protected, allowing businesses to continue innovating without the risk of losing critical competitive advantages.

Encouraging Collaboration: A secure environment enables businesses to collaborate with partners, researchers, and third-party developers without fear of data leakage or IP theft.

Preserving Competitive Edge: By protecting proprietary technologies and processes, security helps companies maintain a leading position in the market as they introduce new products and innovations.

Example: Tesla's strong focus on cybersecurity has helped protect its cutting-edge advancements in autonomous driving and electric vehicle technology, ensuring that competitors and hackers cannot easily replicate their innovations.

4. ENHANCING PRODUCT INNOVATION THROUGH SECURITY FEATURES

Security itself can be a driver of product innovation. As users and businesses become more concerned about data privacy and cybersecurity threats, companies that prioritize security in their products can differentiate themselves from competitors. This has led to a wave of security-focused innovations, particularly in software, IoT devices, and cloud services.

BENEFITS TO INNOVATION:

Differentiation in Competitive Markets: Secure products are seen as more trustworthy, giving companies a competitive advantage and enabling them to charge a premium for security features.

New Revenue Streams: Security features, such as multi-factor authentication (MFA), encryption, and secure access controls, can be offered as value-added services, opening up new revenue streams for businesses.

User-Driven Innovation: Users increasingly demand more control over their privacy and security settings. Meeting these demands drives innovation in areas like data encryption, privacy controls, and security transparency.

Example: Google's development of the Titan Security Key, a physical device that provides enhanced two-factor authentication, is an example of how security concerns can drive product innovation. This security-focused product helps protect users from phishing and other cyberattacks, giving businesses and users greater confidence in their digital interactions.

5. REDUCING DOWNTIME AND OPERATIONAL DISRUPTIONS

Security breaches can be incredibly costly, not just in terms of financial losses but also in terms of downtime and damage to innovative projects. Companies with weak security may face disruptions to operations due to cyberattacks, leading to delays in product launches or the halting of development altogether. By investing in strong security measures, companies can reduce the likelihood of such disruptions, keeping innovation timelines on track.

BENEFITS TO EFFICIENCY:

Minimizing Downtime: A strong security framework reduces the risk of operational disruptions caused by cyberattacks or data breaches, allowing innovation to continue uninterrupted.

Ensuring Business Continuity: With security measures in place, companies can maintain continuity during and after security incidents, ensuring that R&D and product development are not derailed.

Cost Savings: Preventing security breaches saves companies from costly recovery efforts, allowing them to invest more in innovation and development.

Example: Equifax's data breach in 2017, which exposed the personal information of 147 million people, led to significant downtime, lawsuits, and fines. Had stronger security measures been in place, the company could have avoided these costly disruptions and continued focusing on its innovative efforts.

6. ENABLING SCALABILITY IN NEW TECHNOLOGIES

As businesses scale their operations and introduce new technologies, security becomes even more critical. Whether scaling cloud infrastructure, integrating AI-driven systems, or expanding IoT networks, security must be a core consideration to ensure that new technologies are deployed safely and without exposing vulnerabilities.

BENEFITS TO INNOVATION:

Scalable Security Solutions: When security is built into the foundation of new technologies, companies can scale their innovations without increasing the risk of breaches or vulnerabilities.

Seamless Integration of Emerging Technologies: Security ensures that emerging technologies such as blockchain, AI, and quantum computing can be integrated into existing systems without compromising data protection or network integrity.

Supporting Innovation at Scale: With robust security measures in place, companies can confidently innovate and expand into new markets or regions without fear of compromising security standards.

Example: Amazon Web Services (AWS) provides cloud-based security solutions that allow businesses to scale their cloud infrastructure securely. By offering features like encryption, access control, and threat detection, AWS enables companies to innovate in the cloud while ensuring their data and systems are protected.

7. ENCOURAGING REGULATORY COMPLIANCE AND ETHICAL INNOVATION

As global privacy and security regulations become stricter, businesses must ensure that their innovations comply with legal standards. Security is a key enabler of compliance, helping companies adhere to regulations while still fostering innovation. Secure products that meet regulatory requirements also reduce the risk of legal challenges and fines, allowing businesses to innovate responsibly.

BENEFITS TO INNOVATION:

Compliance as a Competitive Advantage: Companies that innovate while complying with security regulations like GDPR and HIPAA can position themselves as leaders in ethical technology, gaining a competitive edge.

Reducing Legal Risks: Compliance with security standards reduces the risk of regulatory penalties, allowing companies to focus on innovation rather than legal battles.

Ethical Innovation: By prioritizing security, companies can ensure their innovations are ethical, protecting user data and privacy in a way that builds long-term trust.

Example: Zoom's rapid rise during the COVID-19 pandemic highlighted the importance of security and compliance. After facing criticism of security lapses, the company invested heavily in improving encryption and data protection, helping it maintain user trust and innovate its platform responsibly.

Security is not an obstacle to innovation but rather its foundation. By integrating security into the core of their development processes, companies can foster a trusted environment where experimentation, collaboration, and scalability can thrive. From protecting intellectual property and enabling safe prototyping to driving product differentiation and ensuring regulatory compliance, strong security practices are essential for any business looking to innovate responsibly and sustainably.

THE ROLE OF ENCRYPTION, AUTHENTICATION, AND REGULAR AUDITS

In an increasingly digital world, ensuring robust security practices is critical for driving innovation and maintaining trust. Encryption, authentication, and regular audits are key pillars that help organizations safeguard their data, protect user privacy, and maintain system integrity. Together, these components ensure that innovation can thrive in a secure and compliant environment.

a. Encryption: Protecting Data Privacy and Integrity

Encryption is the process of converting data into a format that is unreadable to unauthorized users. By using encryption, businesses ensure that sensitive information is kept secure whether it is stored or transmitted, allowing innovation to continue without the fear of data breaches.

ROLE IN SECURITY:

Data Protection: Encryption ensures that sensitive information, such as customer data, intellectual property, and financial transactions, is unreadable to attackers even if it is intercepted.

Compliance with Regulations: Many industries, including finance and healthcare, require data encryption to comply with legal regulations like GDPR, HIPAA, and PCI-DSS.

Ensuring Data Integrity: Encryption ensures that data remains unchanged during transmission or storage, protecting its integrity from tampering or unauthorized modification.

ROLE IN INNOVATION:

Secure Development of Products and Services: Encryption enables businesses to innovate while ensuring user data is protected. For example, encrypted communication apps like WhatsApp and Signal have built successful innovations on secure messaging platforms.

Fostering Trust for Adoption: Encryption helps build trust between users and businesses, which is essential for encouraging the adoption of new technologies.

Example: Financial institutions use end-to-end encryption to secure online banking services and transactions, protecting users' financial data from theft and fraud, while ensuring their confidence in using innovative financial services.

b. Authentication: Ensuring Secure Access Control

Authentication is the process of verifying the identity of users or devices before granting access to data or systems. It acts as the first line of defense in controlling who can access sensitive information and resources.

ROLE IN SECURITY:

Access Control: Strong authentication protocols, such as multi-factor authentication (MFA), ensure that only authorized individuals or systems can access sensitive data or make changes to it.

Preventing Unauthorized Access: Authentication helps protect against data breaches, account takeovers, and insider threats by ensuring that only verified users can interact with sensitive systems.

Protecting Against Phishing and Social Engineering Attacks: With advanced authentication measures, businesses reduce the risk of attacks that rely on stealing login credentials.

ROLE IN INNOVATION:

Supporting Secure Collaboration: Authentication allows businesses to collaborate securely with external partners or clients, ensuring that shared data or systems are accessed only by authorized parties.

Enhancing User Experience: Innovations in authentication, such as biometric login systems (facial recognition, fingerprint scanning), offer both security and convenience, improving the overall user experience.

Example: Tech companies like Google and Apple use multi-factor authentication and biometric authentication (e.g., Face ID and Touch ID) to ensure that users can access their devices and accounts securely while also enhancing the usability of their products.

c. Regular Audits: Ensuring Compliance and Continuous Improvement

Regular security audits involve reviewing an organization's security policies, practices, and infrastructure to identify weaknesses and ensure compliance with security standards. These audits are crucial for maintaining a high level of security over time and supporting sustainable innovation.

ROLE IN SECURITY:

Identifying Vulnerabilities: Regular audits uncover gaps in security measures, such as outdated software or weak access controls, enabling businesses to address vulnerabilities before they are exploited.

Ensuring Regulatory Compliance: Many industries require regular security audits to comply with standards such as ISO 27001, GDPR, and HIPAA. Ensuring compliance helps avoid fines, legal penalties, and reputational damage.

Monitoring System Integrity: Audits help organizations verify the effectiveness of security controls, ensuring that data and systems remain secure and resilient against evolving threats.

ROLE IN INNOVATION:

Encouraging Continuous Improvement: Audits create a culture of accountability and continuous improvement, ensuring that security evolves alongside technological innovations.

Safeguarding New Technologies: Before launching new products or services, audits can validate that security measures are adequate, reducing the risk of vulnerabilities in innovative solutions.

Risk Management for New Projects: Regular audits help assess the security risks associated with new innovations, allowing businesses to address potential threats early in the development process.

Example: Global companies like Amazon and Microsoft conduct regular security audits of their cloud services to ensure compliance with industry standards. These audits help maintain trust in their platforms and ensure the security of new services and innovations.

Encryption, authentication, and regular audits play critical roles in protecting data and systems while enabling secure innovation. Encryption ensures data privacy and integrity, authentication controls access to sensitive information, and regular audits provide a framework for ongoing security improvement and compliance. Together, these practices enable organizations to innovate responsibly while maintaining trust and security in a rapidly evolving digital landscape.

IMPLEMENTING SECURE CODING PRACTICES WITHOUT SACRIFICING EFFICIENCY

Secure coding practices are essential for preventing vulnerabilities and ensuring the security of software applications. However, the challenge for development teams is how to implement these practices without compromising efficiency, speed, or innovation. By embedding security into the software development lifecycle (SDLC) in a streamlined way, teams can maintain productivity while also protecting their systems from threats.

Here's how to implement secure coding practices effectively without sacrificing efficiency:

1. INTEGRATE SECURITY EARLY (SHIFT LEFT)

The principle of "shifting left" refers to incorporating security measures early in the software development process, rather than treating it as an afterthought. When security is considered from the beginning, it becomes part of the overall development flow rather than a separate, time-consuming task.

BEST PRACTICES:

Incorporate Security in the Requirements Phase: Define security requirements alongside functional requirements, ensuring they are part of the project scope.

Use Threat Modeling: Identify potential security threats early and design features to address them during the planning and design stages.

Automate Security Testing: Integrate security checks into continuous integration/continuous deployment (CI/CD) pipelines, so that vulnerabilities are caught as code is written and updated.

BENEFITS:

Less Rework: Addressing security issues early in the SDLC reduces the need for costly rework later, improving overall efficiency.

Faster Time-to-Market: By catching security flaws earlier, teams spend less time addressing them in post-production, speeding up delivery times.

2. LEVERAGE SECURITY AUTOMATION

Manual security testing can be time-consuming and error prone. Automating security checks helps ensure that code is continuously scanned for vulnerabilities, reducing the risk of human error while speeding up the process.

BEST PRACTICES:

Use Static Application Security Testing (SAST): SAST tools analyze source code for security flaws during the development process. This helps developers find and fix issues before the code moves into production.

Dynamic Application Security Testing (DAST): DAST tools scan running applications for vulnerabilities in real-time, ensuring that both code and configuration errors are caught.

Implement Automated Code Reviews: Use tools that automatically review code for common security issues, allowing developers to focus on writing new features rather than spending hours manually testing their work.

BENEFITS:

Increased Coverage: Automation tools can scan large amounts of code faster and more thoroughly than manual testing, improving overall security without slowing down development.

Reduced Manual Workload: Developers spend less time performing repetitive security checks, allowing them to focus on innovation and feature development.

3. ADOPT A SECURITY-FIRST CULTURE

Security should be part of the team's mindset, not a task that's delegated to specific security experts at the end of the process. By promoting a security-first culture within the team, developers are more likely to write secure code as a natural part of their work.

BEST PRACTICES:

Security Training and Education: Provide developers with regular training on secure coding practices, common vulnerabilities (like the OWASP Top 10), and the latest security trends.

Encourage Collaboration with Security Teams: Foster a collaborative environment between development and security teams to encourage open discussions about security concerns.

Incorporate Security into Code Reviews: Make security a standard part of the peer review process, encouraging all team members to spot and fix potential vulnerabilities.

BENEFITS:

Fewer Security Incidents: When developers are aware of security best practices, they write more secure code, reducing the number of vulnerabilities that make it into production.

Faster Issue Resolution: Teams with a security-first mindset are better equipped to address security issues quickly, keeping projects on track.

4. USE SECURE CODING STANDARDS AND LIBRARIES

Standardizing secure coding practices ensures consistency across the team while also streamlining development. Using pre-validated security libraries can reduce the complexity of implementing security measures.

BEST PRACTICES:

Adopt Secure Coding Guidelines: Follow well-established coding standards such as CERT, CWE, or OWASP secure coding guidelines to avoid common security pitfalls.

Use Pre-Approved Security Libraries: Instead of building security functions from scratch, rely on trusted, well-maintained libraries for encryption, authentication, and other security features. This reduces the time and effort required to implement security.

Implement Code Reusability: Develop reusable security modules that can be quickly integrated into different projects, ensuring that security features are implemented consistently without redoing work.

BENEFITS:

Consistency Across Projects: Secure coding standards help teams follow best practices consistently, minimizing security risks without disrupting workflows.

Time Savings: Using trusted libraries and reusable components shortens the development cycle, allowing teams to focus on innovation rather than rebuilding secure features from scratch.

5. IMPLEMENT CONTINUOUS LEARNING AND FEEDBACK LOOPS

Learning from past vulnerabilities and security incidents helps teams continuously improve their coding practices. Feedback loops that allow developers to learn from their mistakes encourage growth without reducing efficiency.

BEST PRACTICES:

Post-Mortem Analysis of Security Incidents: Review security breaches or vulnerabilities after they occur to understand their root causes. Share these learnings across the team to prevent similar issues in the future.

Integrate Security Metrics into Performance Reviews: Track security-related metrics, such as the number of vulnerabilities caught in each development phase and use these as part of the team's performance evaluation. This encourages developers to prioritize security.

Continuous Education: Stay updated on the latest security threats and tools, ensuring the team is aware of emerging vulnerabilities and techniques to address them.

BENEFITS:

Fewer Recurring Vulnerabilities: By learning from past issues, developers are less likely to repeat the same mistakes, reducing the time spent fixing similar vulnerabilities.

Continuous Improvement: Regular feedback ensures the team is always improving its secure coding practices without sacrificing productivity.

6. BALANCE SECURITY WITH PERFORMANCE OPTIMIZATION

Security measures can sometimes introduce performance bottlenecks, particularly in areas like encryption, authentication, or input validation.

Striking the right balance between security and performance ensures that applications remain fast and efficient without compromising security.

BEST PRACTICES:

Optimize Security Features: Ensure that security features like encryption are efficiently implemented to minimize performance overhead. Use algorithms that provide the right balance between security strength and speed.

Measure Performance Impact: Regularly test the performance impact of security features and identify optimizations to improve speed without sacrificing security.

Prioritize Security Where It Matters Most: Focus on high-risk areas (e.g., data handling, user authentication) to avoid over-engineering security in low-risk areas where it may slow down development without significant benefit.

BENEFITS:

Faster Performance: Optimized security implementations allow for both high performance and strong protection.

Improved User Experience: Balancing security with performance ensures that users are protected without experiencing lag or slow response times.

Secure coding practices can be implemented without sacrificing efficiency by integrating security early, leveraging automation, fostering a security-first culture, and using trusted libraries and standards. By embedding security into every phase of the development process and focusing on continuous learning, development teams can build secure, high-quality software efficiently, without delays or bottlenecks. This approach helps businesses protect their systems and data while continuing to innovate.

CHAPTER 9

SOFTWARE DEVELOPMENT METRICS AND PERFOMANCE OPTIMISATIONS

Software development is a complex process that requires careful planning, execution, and monitoring to ensure that projects are completed on time, within budget, and with high quality. To achieve these goals, it's essential to measure progress, productivity, and performance through key metrics. Furthermore, performance optimization ensures that the final product meets user expectations in terms of speed, efficiency, and scalability.

IMPORTANCE OF SOFTWARE DEVELOPMENT METRICS

Metrics serve as quantitative tools that help teams measure the effectiveness and efficiency of their development processes. By tracking the right metrics, teams can identify bottlenecks, monitor progress, and ensure that the software aligns with business goals.

KEY BENEFITS OF SOFTWARE DEVELOPMENT METRICS:

Visibility: Metrics provide insight into developmental progress, allowing stakeholders to monitor whether teams are on track.

Accountability: Teams are held accountable by tracking performance, making it easier to identify areas for improvement.

Continuous Improvement: Data-driven insights help identify inefficiencies and enable continuous process improvements.

Risk Management: Metrics allow teams to detect potential issues early, such as scope creep or technical debt, and take corrective actions before they become critical problems.

KEY PERFORMANCE INDICATORS (KPIS) FOR MEASURING EFFICIENCY AND INNOVATION

When measuring efficiency and innovation, KPIs must be tailored to the specific goals and nature of the business or project. Below are some common KPIs for both categories:

Efficiency KPIs

A. OPERATIONAL EFFICIENCY:

Cost per unit produced: Measures the cost incurred to produce each unit.

Production time per unit: The time taken to produce one unit of product or deliver a service.

Resource Utilization: Tracks how effectively resources (e.g., labor, materials) are used.

Cycle Time: The total time taken from the start to the completion of a process.

Throughput: Measures the output of production or services over a given time period.

Employee Productivity: Tracks the amount of output per employee.

B. CUSTOMER SATISFACTION:

First Response Time: Measures how quickly customer service responds to queries.

Net Promoter Score (NPS): Gauges customer loyalty and the likelihood of recommending your product or service.

Customer Retention Rate: Tracks how many customers return over a given time period.

Customer Acquisition Cost (CAC): The cost associated with acquiring a new customer.

C. FINANCIAL EFFICIENCY:

Operating Margin: Measures profitability as a percentage of revenue.

Return on Investment (ROI): Indicates how much profit is made relative to the amount invested.

Cash Flow Efficiency: Tracks how well a company is managing its cash flow to cover its obligations.

D. PROCESS EFFICIENCY:

Defect Rate: The percentage of products or services with defects.

Order Fulfillment Cycle Time: Time from order placement to delivery.

Inventory Turnover: How quickly inventory is sold and replaced over a period.

Innovation KPIs

i. Idea Generation:

Number of New Ideas Submitted: The total number of ideas generated by employees or teams.

Idea Implementation Rate: The percentage of ideas that are turned into actionable projects.

Employee Participation in Innovation Initiatives: Tracks how many employees contribute to innovation programs.

ii. Time to Market:

Time from Concept to Launch: Measures the speed of transforming an idea into a market-ready product.

Time to Prototype: The duration taken to develop a working prototype.

iii. Revenue from New Products/Services:

The percentage of total revenue generated from products or services introduced within the last few years.

iv. R&D Spending:

Percentage of Revenue Spent on R&D: How much of the company's revenue is reinvested into research and development.

Number of Patents Filed: Tracks the number of patents registered by the organization.

v. Market Adoption:

Market Penetration: The percentage of a target market that has adopted a new product or service.

Customer Feedback on New Products: Tracks satisfaction and usage rates for new innovations.

vi. Innovation Success Rate:

Percentage of Innovations Successfully Brought to Market: Tracks how many new ideas are successfully commercialized or adopted.

These KPIs can be adapted and customized to fit the specific objectives of your business, and help you measure both efficiency and the success of innovative initiatives.

HOW TO USE DATA AND ANALYTICS TO REFINE SOFTWARE PROJECTS

Using data and analytics to refine software projects is essential for improving efficiency, user experience, and overall project success. Here's a step-by-step approach:

A. DEFINE KEY METRICS AND GOALS

Set Clear Objectives: Start by identifying what you want to achieve with your software project. Common goals include improving performance, enhancing user experience, or reducing bugs.

Identify KPIs: Choose key performance indicators (KPIs) that align with your goals. For example, tracking page load time, user retention rates, or customer satisfaction.

B. DATA COLLECTION

User Data: Capture how users interact with the software through tools like Google Analytics, Mixpanel, or custom logging. This can include user journeys, click paths, feature usage, and drop-off points.

Performance Data: Collect metrics on software performance, such as response times, server loads, error rates, and downtime. Tools like New Relic, DataDog, or open-source tools can provide these insights.

Feedback and Surveys: Use customer feedback tools (e.g., NPS surveys or feedback forms) to gather user opinions on the software's functionality and usability.

A/B Testing Data: If you are experimenting with new features or design elements, track performance through A/B tests to see which version yields better results.

C. DATA ANALYSIS

User Behavior Analysis: Use data to understand how users interact with your software, where they encounter problems, and which features are most popular. Heatmaps and session recordings (e.g., Hotjar or Crazy Egg) help visualize user interactions.

Performance Analytics: Analyze performance data to identify inefficiencies like slow response times or memory leaks. This can be done using analytics dashboards and performance monitoring tools.

Error and Crash Reports: Tools like Sentry or Rollbar help you analyze error logs and crash reports to determine the root cause of bugs and issues.

D. DATA-DRIVEN DECISION MAKING

Feature Prioritization: Use analytics to determine which features are most frequently used and which are underutilized. Prioritize developing or improving features based on user engagement.

Optimize User Flows: Based on user interaction data, streamline the user journey to reduce friction. For example, if users drop off at a particular stage in a sign-up process, you can optimize that step.

Performance Optimization: Identify bottlenecks in system performance through data, such as slow queries or high memory usage, and address them accordingly.

Bug Fixes and Stability: Focus on fixing bugs that affect the largest percentage of users by analyzing crash reports and error logs.

E. PREDICTIVE ANALYTICS

Forecast User Behavior: Use machine learning models to predict future user behavior based on historical data. For example, identifying users at risk of churning based on their activity patterns.

Use data to anticipate demand for new features or software improvements, allowing you to allocate resources accordingly.

Capacity Planning: Analyze usage patterns to predict traffic spikes and ensure infrastructure can handle increased loads.

F. A/B TESTING AND EXPERIMENTATION

Test New Features: Use A/B testing to compare different versions of features, designs, or workflows. Analyze results to determine which variant provides the best performance and user satisfaction.

Continuous Iteration: Run experiments continuously to refine the software based on real-world data. Analytics platforms can help you track the results of your tests in real time.

G. USER SEGMENTATION AND PERSONALIZATION

Segment Users: Break down users into segments (e.g., power users, new users, inactive users) to understand their different needs and behaviors. Tailor the software experience to suit different user types.

Personalized Features: Based on data insights, create personalized experiences for different user groups, such as recommending certain features or content based on their previous interactions.

H. CONTINUOUS MONITORING AND FEEDBACK LOOP

Real-time Monitoring: Set up dashboards and alerts for key metrics to identify problems or areas for improvement as they occur. Use tools like Grafana, Kibana, or Tableau for data visualization.

Feedback Loop: Establish a feedback loop where data is continually collected and analyzed, and improvements are continuously rolled out based on insights. Implement agile methodologies to ensure rapid iteration and refinement.

i. Automate Data Processes

Automated Reporting: Create automated reports and dashboards that provide real-time data insights to stakeholders, allowing quicker decision-making.

Automated Alerts: Set up automatic alerts for critical issues, such as performance degradation or security vulnerabilities, so the development team can address them quickly.

By leveraging data and analytics, you can make informed decisions at every stage of a software project, leading to improved user experience, better performance, and overall project success.

MEASURING SUCCESS BEYOND CODE IMPACT ON BUSINESS OUTCOMES

Measuring success beyond code focuses on how software projects contribute to broader business outcomes and value creation. While technical metrics are important, true success is reflected in the project's impact on customer satisfaction, revenue growth, and overall strategic goals. Here's how you can assess success beyond the code:

A. BUSINESS OBJECTIVES ALIGNMENT

Contribution to Business Goals: Measure how the software aligns with and contributes to overall business objectives, such as market expansion, customer acquisition, or operational efficiency.

Example: If the goal is to increase customer acquisition, track how the software enables a new lead generation or simplifies the customer onboarding process.

B. CUSTOMER SATISFACTION AND ENGAGEMENT

Customer Satisfaction (CSAT): Use surveys and feedback tools to gauge user satisfaction. Track CSAT scores to understand how happy users are with the product.

Net Promoter Score (NPS): Measure how likely customers are to recommend your product. A higher NPS indicates greater user loyalty, which positively impacts business growth.

User Engagement: Monitor user activity within the software, such as active daily/weekly users, time spent on the platform, and feature usage. High engagement typically correlates with business success, as it indicates value delivery.

Churn Rate: Track the percentage of users or customers who stop using the software. A low churn rate signifies strong customer retention, directly contributing to sustained revenue.

C. REVENUE IMPACT

Revenue Growth: Measure the impact of the software on business revenue. This includes direct contributions (e.g., sales through the platform) and indirect impacts (e.g., software automating tasks that lead to cost savings or enabling new business models).

Example: If the software platform supports a subscription model, track how new features increase subscriber numbers or reduce cancellations.

Cost Reduction: Evaluate how the software contributes to reducing operational costs, such as automation of repetitive tasks, improved supply chain management, or better resource allocation.

D. MARKET AND COMPETITIVE POSITION

Market Penetration: Assess how the software has helped the company capture a larger share of the market. This could be measured by new customer acquisitions, entering new geographical regions, or serving a previously untapped audience.

Competitive Advantage: Analyze how the software differentiates the business from competitors. This can be based on unique features, better customer experience, or faster time to market, which strengthen the business's competitive edge.

E. OPERATIONAL EFFICIENCY

Process Automation and Optimization: Evaluate how the software has improved business operations by automating workflows, reducing errors, or optimizing resource use. Efficiency gains should lead to higher productivity and cost savings.

Employee Productivity: Measure the impact of the software on employee performance. If the software enhances collaboration, reduces manual work, or provides better insights, it leads to improved productivity across teams.

Example: Implementing a CRM software that reduces time spent on administrative tasks, allowing sales teams to focus more on closing deals.

F. INNOVATION AND STRATEGIC GROWTH

New Product/Service Offerings: Track how the software enables the creation of new products or services that drive business growth. This can be an expansion into new digital offerings or enhancement of existing ones.

Agility and Flexibility: Evaluate how the software enables the business to pivot quickly in response to market changes. This includes faster feature rollouts, adaptable architectures, or a better understanding of customer needs.

Example: A company like Flexibiz can adapt its platform to new market demands based on customer feedback and data analytics.

G. CUSTOMER ACQUISITION AND RETENTION

Customer Lifetime Value (CLTV): Measure the total revenue generated by a customer over the entire duration of their relationship with the business. If the software improves customer experience and satisfaction, CLTV should increase.

Customer Acquisition Cost (CAC): Track how much it costs to acquire a new customer through the software. If the software makes the sales process more efficient or provides valuable data for marketing, CAC should decrease.

H. BRAND PERCEPTION AND MARKET INFLUENCE

Brand Equity: Monitor how the software affects brand perception. Positive user experiences with the software can improve the company's reputation and strengthen brand loyalty.

Social media and Public Sentiment: Analyze social media mentions, reviews, and public feedback to gauge how the software impacts public perception of the business. Positive feedback can lead to greater trust and credibility in the market.

I. SCALABILITY AND FUTURE READINESS

Scalability: Assess the software's ability to scale with business growth. This includes technical scalability (e.g., handling increased user loads) and business scalability (e.g., enabling the business to expand into new markets without significant operational bottlenecks).

Adaptability to Future Needs: Measure how future proof the software is by evaluating its architecture, flexibility, and ability to support new technologies or business models.

J. REGULATORY AND COMPLIANCE BENEFITS

Compliance and Risk Management: Evaluate how the software supports regulatory compliance, such as data privacy or industry-specific regulations. Ensuring compliance reduces legal risks, protects the company's reputation, and avoids costly penalties.

By focusing on these business outcomes, you can go beyond technical success and measure how software development efforts contribute to strategic goals, financial performance, and long-term business growth. This approach provides a holistic view of success, integrating both technical excellence and business value creation.

CHAPTER 10

FUTURE TRENDS IN SOFTWARE DEVELOPMENT

The future of software development is characterized by the convergence of emerging technologies like AI, quantum computing, blockchain, and AR/VR, with an emphasis on ethical practices, sustainability, and user-centric design. Developers will need to continuously adapt to these innovations, embrace automation, and adopt new tools and frameworks that prioritize flexibility, security, and scalability. Ultimately, the success of software projects will be measured by their ability to drive meaningful business outcomes while staying aligned with the future needs of both users and society at large.

Below are the key trends that will likely define the future of software development:

A. ARTIFICIAL INTELLIGENCE (AI) AND MACHINE LEARNING (ML) INTEGRATION

AI-Augmented Development: AI tools are being increasingly integrated into development workflows to automate coding, detect bugs, and suggest improvements. Platforms like GitHub Copilot and OpenAI's Codex offer developers real-time assistance by writing or completing code based on context.

Predictive Analytics in Software: AI can analyze large datasets to predict future behaviors or trends, which can be applied to create more personalized and intelligent software solutions.

Automated Testing: AI-driven testing tools will reduce manual testing effort, identifying patterns, bugs, and security vulnerabilities more effectively.

B. LOW-CODE AND NO-CODE PLATFORMS

Democratization of Software Development: Low-code and no-code platforms enable non-technical users to build applications using graphical interfaces and pre-built templates. This trend is empowering more people to create software, accelerating digital transformation across industries.

Faster Prototyping and Deployment: These platforms allow businesses to quickly prototype and deploy applications, significantly shortening development cycles and reducing costs.

C. EDGE COMPUTING AND 5G

Decentralized Processing: With the growth of edge computing, data processing will happen closer to the data source (e.g., IoT devices, autonomous cars), reducing latency and improving performance. This will influence the design and deployment of software that relies on real-time processing.

5G Connectivity: The rollout of 5G networks will enable ultra-fast data transmission, fostering the development of high-bandwidth applications, such as augmented reality (AR), virtual reality (VR), and autonomous vehicles.

D. QUANTUM COMPUTING

Next-Generation Problem Solving: Quantum computing promises to solve problems that are currently infeasible with classical computers. As this technology matures, software developers will need to adapt to new quantum algorithms and programming languages to harness its power.

Quantum-Safe Encryption: As quantum computers develop, they will have the potential to break current encryption methods. Software will need to evolve to integrate quantum-safe cryptography, ensuring data security in a quantum future.

E. CLOUD-NATIVE DEVELOPMENT AND MICROSERVICES

Cloud-Native Architectures: Software development is moving toward cloud-native approaches, with applications designed specifically to leverage the scalability, resilience, and flexibility of cloud environments.

Microservices Architecture: The shift from monolithic architectures to microservices allows software to be broken down into smaller, independent components. This increases development speed, improves scalability, and enables continuous deployment.

Serverless Computing: Developers are increasingly using serverless architectures, where cloud providers manage the infrastructure. This trend allows developers to focus solely on writing code without worrying about infrastructure management.

F. BLOCKCHAIN AND DECENTRALIZED APPLICATIONS (DAPPS)

Blockchain-Based Software: Blockchain technology is moving beyond cryptocurrencies and finding applications in secure, transparent software development. Blockchain can be used to enhance security, create decentralized apps (dApps), and enable smart contracts.

Digital Identity and Data Ownership: Blockchain may play a significant role in future software that enables decentralized data ownership, allowing users to have more control over their personal data.

G. AUGMENTED REALITY (AR) AND VIRTUAL REALITY (VR)

Immersive Software Experiences: AR and VR technologies are becoming more sophisticated, allowing for immersive user experiences in gaming, education, healthcare, and e-commerce.

Metaverse Development: As companies like Meta (formerly Facebook) invest heavily in the metaverse, developers will focus on creating interconnected virtual worlds where users interact in real-time, creating entirely new industries and business models.

H. SUSTAINABILITY IN SOFTWARE DEVELOPMENT

Green Software Engineering: As businesses prioritize sustainability, software development will follow suit. Green software engineering focuses on creating energy-efficient code, optimizing infrastructure to minimize power consumption, and adopting sustainable development practices.

Eco-Friendly Cloud Solutions: Cloud providers are starting to offer green computing solutions that use renewable energy sources and energy-efficient data centers, reducing the environmental impact of software.

I. DEVOPS AND CONTINUOUS EVERYTHING

Continuous Integration and Continuous Delivery (CI/CD): DevOps practices will continue to evolve, enabling even faster and more reliable software delivery. Automation in testing, deployment, and monitoring will streamline development cycles.

GitOps and Infrastructure as Code: These practices will become more mainstream, enabling developers to manage infrastructure through code. This results in more consistent, scalable, and repeatable deployments across environments.

Observability and AIOps: As systems become more complex, monitoring, logging, and analytics will rely on AI and automation to provide real-time insights and proactive issue detection.

J. ETHICAL SOFTWARE DEVELOPMENT

Responsible AI and Data Privacy: As AI and automation become more pervasive, ethical considerations around data privacy, bias, and security will be increasingly important. Developers will need to prioritize transparency, fairness, and accountability in their solutions.

Open-Source Ethics: Open-source software will continue to grow in importance, but developers and organizations must focus on maintaining the ethical use of open-source projects and ensuring proper security and governance.

K. HUMAN-CENTERED DESIGN AND USER EXPERIENCE (UX)

AI-Enhanced UX: AI will play a larger role in designing more personalized and intuitive user interfaces, learning from user interactions to continuously improve the user experience.

Voice and Gesture Interfaces: The future of user interfaces may move beyond the keyboard and screen, with software increasingly integrating voice commands, gesture recognition, and even brain-computer interfaces (BCIs).

L. CYBERSECURITY AND PRIVACY BY DESIGN

Zero-Trust Security Models: As cyber threats become more sophisticated, the zero-trust model will become a standard approach, where every user or system component is continuously authenticated and verified.

Privacy by Design: New software will need to be built with data privacy at its core, ensuring compliance with global regulations (e.g., GDPR) and prioritizing user data protection from the beginning of development.

THE IMPORTANCE OF UPSKILLING AND ADAPTING TO NEW TOOLS AND FRAMEWORKS

Upskilling and adapting to new tools and frameworks are vital for both personal career growth and organizational success. In a fast-paced industry like software development, professionals who commit to continuous learning are better equipped to deliver high-quality, innovative solutions and stay ahead of the competition. By embracing lifelong learning, developers can future proof their careers and play a pivotal role in shaping the next generation of software solutions. Below are key reasons why continuous learning and adaptability being essential:

A. STAYING RELEVANT IN A FAST-CHANGING INDUSTRY

Technological Evolution: Software development is one of the fastest-evolving industries, with new languages, frameworks, and tools constantly emerging. Upskilling ensures that developers stay up to date with the latest technologies and best practices.

Avoiding Skill Obsolescence: Skills that were cutting-edge just a few years ago can quickly become outdated. Regularly updating technical knowledge helps professionals avoid falling behind and becoming less competitive in the job market.

B. ENHANCED PROBLEM-SOLVING ABILITIES

Access to Better Tools: New tools and frameworks often come with improved functionalities that simplify complex tasks, enhance productivity, and make problem-solving more efficient. Being proficient in modern tools allows developers to solve problems faster and more effectively.

Broadening Skillset: Learning new languages or frameworks can broaden a developer's toolkit. With a wider array of skills, developers can approach challenges from different perspectives and find better solutions to diverse problems.

C. INCREASED PRODUCTIVITY AND EFFICIENCY

Leveraging Automation: Modern development tools often automate repetitive tasks such as testing, code deployment, and debugging. By adopting these tools, developers can significantly reduce time spent on manual processes and focus on more critical aspects of development.

Faster Development Cycles: New frameworks, such as those designed for agile and DevOps environments, enable faster iterations and continuous integration. This boosts productivity and ensures that development teams can deliver features and updates in shorter timeframes.

D. IMPROVED SOFTWARE QUALITY AND PERFORMANCE

Optimized for New Standards: As development practices evolve, new tools and frameworks are often designed to meet higher standards in terms of security, performance, and scalability. Upskilling allows developers to build more secure, efficient, and reliable software.

Adopting Best Practices: Staying up to date with the latest frameworks ensures that developers are following current best practices, which often result in cleaner, more maintainable code and fewer technical issues down the line.

E. ADAPTABILITY TO MARKET DEMANDS

Meeting Client and Market Expectations: Businesses and clients increasingly expect cutting-edge solutions. Developers who can leverage the latest technologies are more likely to meet client demands and stay ahead of competitors.

Supporting Innovation: Innovation thrives when developers are equipped with modern tools. For example, technologies like AI, blockchain, and microservices architectures require new skill sets, and those who upskill in these areas can drive innovation and create differentiated products.

F. CAREER GROWTH AND OPPORTUNITIES

Higher Demand for Modern Skills: Employers are constantly looking for developers who are proficient in the latest technologies. Upskilling makes professionals more attractive in the job market, opening doors to higher-paying roles, promotions, and career advancements.

Freelance and Consulting Opportunities: Developers who continuously update their skills are in a better position to pursue freelance work or consulting roles. Companies often seek specialized skills in newer technologies that in-house teams may lack.

G. SUPPORTING TEAM COLLABORATION AND AGILE WORKFLOWS

Cross-Functional Collaboration: In modern software development, developers often work closely with designers, data scientists, and other departments. Upskilling helps them better understand the tools and technologies used by other teams, leading to improved collaboration.

Agile and DevOps Practices: New frameworks often align with agile and DevOps methodologies, which emphasize continuous delivery and collaboration between development and operations. Adapting to these workflows ensures smoother teamwork and faster iteration cycles.

I. GREATER INNOVATION AND CREATIVITY

Exploring New Approaches: Learning new tools and frameworks exposes developers to alternative ways of thinking and solving problems. This enhances creativity and enables innovation in software solutions.

Expanding Capabilities: Upskilling with tools like machine learning libraries or blockchain frameworks empowers developers to create innovative products that would otherwise be outside their technical scope.

J. FOSTERING A LEARNING CULTURE

Continuous Improvement: In organizations, upskilling not only benefits individuals but also fosters a culture of continuous improvement. Teams that prioritize learning are more likely to innovate and remain competitive.

Encouraging Mentorship and Knowledge Sharing: Developers who regularly update their skills can mentor others, driving collective learning and growth across teams. This helps in maintaining a strong knowledge base within the organization.

www.ingramcontent.com/pod-product-compliance
Lightning Source LLC
LaVergne TN
LVHW092007090526
838202LV00001B/34